Year 1 Contents

To the student

Everyone loves to write. We write lists to remember things. We write notes and emails to our friends. We write stories and poems, reports and recounts.

When we write, we use **words**. We need to know how to spell the words, so that our reader knows what we are writing about. All our words are made up of **letters**.

In the English alphabet, there are 26 letters—**21 consonants** and **5 vowels**.

a b c d e f g h i j k l m

n o p q r s t u v w x y z

Each letter has a **name** and each letter represents a spoken **sound**. Most **consonants** only have one 'sound'. The **vowels** have a number of different 'sounds'.

Spelling is closely linked to **grammar** (the way we put our sentences together). In this book, you will learn how words look and sound. You will also learn how and when to add endings to words, so that what you write sounds right and makes sense. You will learn any spelling rules that apply. The Top 3 rules are on the back page.

Common endings: -s, -es, -ing, -ed, -y, -er, -est

About the author

Del has enjoyed a long career in education as a specialist teacher (Learning Difficulties), education adviser and regional coordinator (English). She has written extensively for parents, teachers and students and is a well-known and respected author nationally and internationally. Her publications cover a diverse range of print and electronic materials in English grammar, spelling, reading, writing and comprehension. She is the author of the popular *Reading Quest* books, a series of readers written for the older, reluctant reader.

Among her latest works are *Blake's Guide to Comprehension*, *Blake's Grammar and Punctuation Guide for lower primary students* and *Targeting Grammar*.

How to Use This Book

Your *Targeting Spelling Activity Book* is set out in units. Each unit contains two word lists.

SEE & SAY

cat	can
hat	man
sat	ran

SEE & SAY

The words in this list target a particular spelling skill. Look at these words and say them aloud several times. Say the last sound in each word loudly. This will help you to remember what the whole word looks like, and what it sounds like. The *See and Say* words provide a warm-up for the activities that follow.

I
am
the

LOOK & LEARN

These words are used all the time in writing to hold ideas together. They often never change their spelling, no matter where you place them in a text. Learn these words with your eyes, like this:

1. Write the word in large letters on a piece of paper or a whiteboard.
2. Look at the word and say it three times.
3. Close your eyes and picture the word.
4. Open your eyes and check. Is the word the same as your picture?
5. Close your eyes and picture the word again. **Write it in the air with your finger.**
6. Check. Is that the word you wrote?
7. Now, cover the word and write it again from your memory.
8. Check. If the word is not correct, go back to Step 2 and try again.

MEMORY TRAINING Spelling is a skill that requires you to remember the words you want to write. Throughout this book, you will be asked to write as many words as you can remember from memory. This will help you to focus on what words look and sound like. Very soon, the words will start to roll off the end of your pencil!

The more you write, the better your spelling will be.

Short Vowels: a

a is a short, snappy sound.
Feel the corners of your mouth stretch
as you say these words:
***a**nt, **a**xe, **a**pple, c**a**t, fl**a**g, c**a**mp.*

SEE & SAY

cat	can
hat	man
sat	ran

LOOK & LEARN

I
am
the

1 Name the pictures.

2 Circle the pictures that begin with the letter in the box.

BOOK 1 - TARGETING SPELLING 1 © PASCAL PRESS ISBN 9781925490190

Practise writing the letter a. Start at the dot •

Many words have the same **stem**.

c	at
h	at
s	at

These are *rhyming words*.

MEMORY TRAINING

- Say each list of words three times.
- How many can you remember?
- Write them in your notebook. Check.
- Write your scores here.

....

Write these *rhyming words*.

c	at	m	an
f		p	
b		f	
m		t	
r		v	

Use the list words above to name these pictures.

I am can be written as ***I'm***.

Examples: ***I am*** *a boy.* → ***I'm*** *a boy.* ***I am*** *six.* → ***I'm*** *six.*

I am *a girl.* → ***I'm*** *a girl.* ***I'm*** *six too.*

UNIT 2

Short Vowels: e

e is a short, snappy sound.
It is the sound you feel in the back of your throat as you say these words:
egg, elf, elephant, get, tent, well.

SEE & SAY

pet	bed
get	red
let	fed

LOOK & LEARN

my
see
like

1 Choose words from the *See and Say* list to complete each sentence.

I put on my **r**_____ cap to go to school.

I **f**_____ my **p**_____ dog with water and dog food.

It is time to **g**_____ into **b**_____ and go to sleep.

Dad **l**_____ the pigs out of the pen.

2 Write the *rhyming words* from the word wheels.

et: w, s, n, v, m, j

en: m, t, h, p, th, d

_____ _____ _____ _____

_____ _____ _____ _____

_____ _____ _____ _____

TARGETING SPELLING 1 © PASCAL PRESS ISBN 9781925490190

Practise writing the letter e. Start at the dot ●

e

Many words are the *names* of things.
They are called **nouns**.
Examples: hat, man, bed, cat, peg

Circle the words that are *nouns*.

hat	am	hen	bat	like
pet	the	my	net	bed

A **plural noun** names *more than one thing*.
To make a noun plural, add **-s** most of the time.
Examples: hen, hens; cat, cats.

Write these nouns in *plural* form (more than one).

hen ________ bag ________ bed ________

bell ________ fan ________ leg ________

Add the missing *vowels*. Choose from a and e.

C__n you see **sh__lls** on the **s__nd**?

The **h__ns** in the **p__n** want to be **f__d**.

My **dr__ss** is **r__d** and so is my **h__t**.

Short Vowels: i

i is a short, snappy sound.
It is the sound you hear when you bring your shoulders up to your ears as you say these words: *in*, *it*, *ill*, *pig*, *slip*, *brick*.

SEE & SAY

did	will
lid	hill
hid	fill

LOOK & LEARN

we
go
to

Choose words from the *See and Say* list to complete the sentences.

Water will **f**_____ the tank if it rains.

D_____ you see a car coming down the **h**_____?

W_____ you play ball with me?

Lift the **l**_____ of the box and look inside.

I **h**_____ Mum's gift under my bed.

2 Write the *rhyming words* on these word ladders.

pin	hit	pig
b	b	b
f	f	f
t	s	d
w	k	w

MEMORY TRAINING

- Say each list of words three times.
- How many can you remember?
- Write them in your notebook. Check.
- Write your scores here.

....

TARGETING SPELLING 1 © PASCAL PRESS ISBN 9781925490190

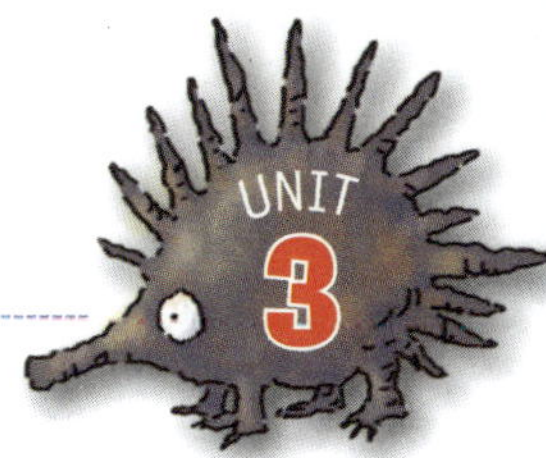

Practise writing the letter i. Start at the dot •

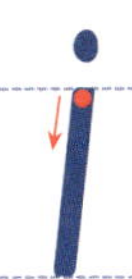

Name the pictures.

Write these nouns in *plural* form (more than one).

pin	______	peg	______	cat	______
pig	______	pet	______	van	______
bin	______	bed	______	bag	______

Mend the broken words to match the pictures. Choose from a, e or i.

h_t	l_d	b_d	h_ll	m_n	sh_ll

Write an ending for each sentence.

We go to ______________________________.

I like to ______________________________.

Did you see the ______________________________?

Short Vowels: o

o is a short, snappy sound.
It is the sound where you make your mouth round like a letter 'o' as you say these words: ***o**ff*, ***o**dd*, ***o**range*, *p**o**t*, *d**o**g*, *m**o**p*.

SEE & SAY

got	dog
hot	log
not	fog

LOOK & LEARN

on
it
is

1 Choose words from the *See and Say* list to complete the sentences.

I **g**____ a little **d**____ for my birthday.

The men got lost in the **f**____.

My **d**____ jumped over a big **l**____.

Do **n**____ put your hand on a **h**____ stove.

MEMORY TRAINING

- Say the words three times.
- How many can you remember?
- Write them in your notebook. Check.
- Write your score here.

....

2 Write the *rhyming words* from the word wheel.

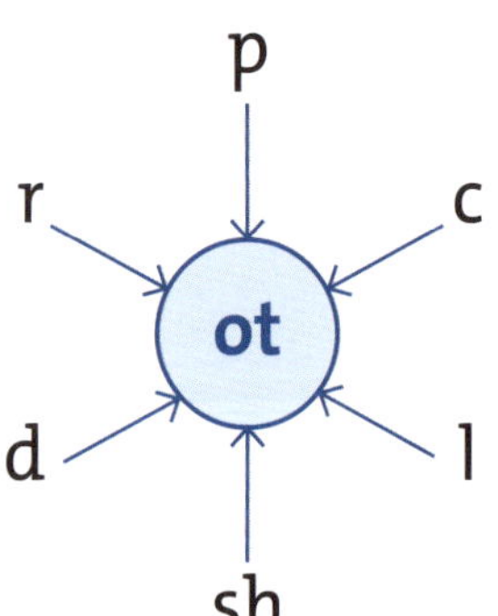

____

____

____

____

____

____

3 Write the pairs of *rhyming words*.

top	rod	box	jog	toss
h____	n____	f____	b____	b____

TARGETING SPELLING 1 © PASCAL PRESS ISBN 9781925490190

Practise writing the letter o. Start at the dot ●

Mend the broken words.

d _ ll	b _ d	z _ _	f _ _
_ _ t	_ _ n	_ _ _	_ _ _

Add **-es** to **nouns** *ending in* ***s*** and ***x*** to make them **plural**. *Examples: bus, **buses**; box, **boxes***

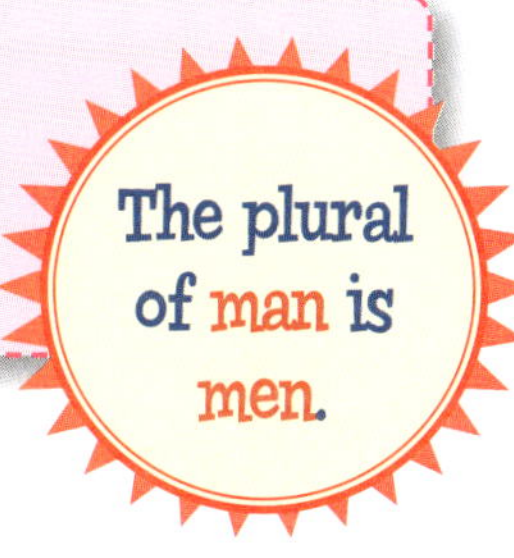

Write these nouns in *plural* form (more than one).

log fox doll pot boss

________ ________ ________ ________ ________

Some words have **opposite** meanings. *Examples: **fast** and **slow**; **old** and **new**; **long** and **short**; **up** and **down***

Colour the pairs of words that are *opposite* in meaning. Use a different colour for each pair.

cold	happy	little	dry	thin	good
thick	wet	sad	hot	bad	big

It is can be written as it's.
Examples:
It is mine. → It's mine.
It is a pig. → It's a pig.
It is hot. → It's hot.

Short Vowels: u

UNIT 5

u is a short, snappy sound.
It is the sound you hear when you drop your jaw as you say these words: ***up***, ***us***, ***under***, ***rug***, ***bus***, ***cup***.

(Place your hands under your jaw like a letter **u**. Drop your hands as you drop your jaw.)

SEE & SAY

sun	cut
fun	nut
run	but

LOOK & LEARN

he
she
me

1 Choose words from the *See and Say* list to complete each sentence.

We had **f**____ playing ball in the park.

It is hot sitting in the **s**____.

I like to **r**____ and jump in the sand.

Mum **c**____ up some **n**____**s** to go in the cake.

MEMORY TRAINING

- Say the words three times.
- How many can you remember?
- Write them in your notebook. Check.
- Write your score here.

....

2 Write the *rhyming words*.

bug	p
t	d
r	h
m	j

3 Name the pictures.

bu__	su__	j__ __	__ __ __	__ __ __	__ __ __

TARGETING SPELLING 1 © PASCAL PRESS ISBN 9781925490190

Practise writing the letter u. Start at the dot •

u

Write the *rhyming words*.

t**ub**	h**um**	m**ud**	r**ut**	s**un**
c___	g___	c___	j___	b___
r___	m___	b___	h___	g___

Pronouns *take the place of* **nouns**. ***He***, ***she*** and ***me*** are pronouns.
Examples: Jack = ***he****; Jill =* ***she***
Jack *is a boy.* ***He*** *likes to play chess.* ***Jill*** *is a girl.* ***She*** *likes to read books. "Read your book to* ***me****,"* ***Jack*** *said.*

Write a *pronoun* in place of the nouns in **bold**.

Katy is in Year 1. _____ likes to do sums.

Dylan is tall. _____ is taller than me.

Mum said, "Give _____ your hand, Ling."

Dad said, "Come to the park with _____."

Add the missing *letters* to match the words and pictures.

t _ _	_ _ ll	_ _ _	_ _ _	_ _ _

Write these nouns in *plural* form (more than one).

cup	nut	mug	bun	cub
________	________	________	________	________

UNIT 6

Letter Teams: ck

c and k go together *at the end* of a word. They have *one* sound, 'c'. It is the sound you hear as you say these words: *back*, *tick*, *lock*, *duck*.

SEE & SAY

back	sock	duck
pack	rock	luck

LOOK & LEARN

mum
and
dad

1 Write the words under the pictures.

I can see   in the pond.

________ ________

I put my 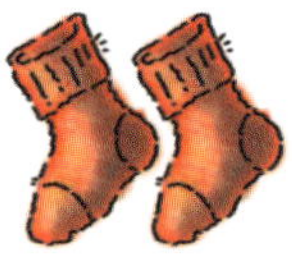 out in the  to dry.

________ ________

Ben has a 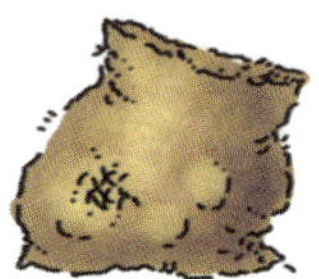 of food for his  .

________ ________

2 Write the *rhyming words*.

kick	nick
t	s
l	w
p	qu

MEMORY TRAINING

- Say the words three times.
- How many can you remember?
- Write them in your notebook. Check.
- Write your score here. ....

RULE

The letters q and u are *always together* in a word. *Examples:* ***quick, quit, queen, quack***

TARGETING SPELLING 1 © PASCAL PRESS ISBN 9781925490190

Write these nouns in *plural* form (more than one).

duck ________ rat ________ hill ________

hand ________ nut ________ rock ________

Spell the missing words. *(Hint: They all end in ck.)*

Here is the key to **l**______ the door.

A giraffe has a long **n**______.

I put on my **s**______**s** and shoes for school.

The **d**______**s** in the pond go **qu**______, **qu**______.

Some words say what people *do*. These *doing words* are called **verbs**. *Examples:* ***run, play, hop, jump***

Pick a *verb* from the box to complete each sentence.

kick	pack	rock	pick

Mum will ________ the baby to sleep.

I will ________ my lunch for school.

Tom can ________ a ball very high.

I will ________ an apple from the apple tree.

Add ck to end these words. Say them three times.

p	e	

b	u	

d	o	

s	u	

Letter Teams: sh, ch

sh makes *one* sound. It is the sound you hear as you say these words: ***shop***, ***ship***, ***fish***, ***dish***.

ch makes *one* sound. It is the sound you hear as you say these words: ***chop***, ***chip***, ***rich***, ***much***.

SEE & SAY

shop	chop
shut	chin
dish	much

LOOK & LEARN

yes
no
look

1 Change the *last sound* to make new words.

shop	fish	chip	much
sho___	fi___	chi___	mu___

2 Write the *rhyming words* on these word ladders.

mash	look	and
l	b	b
c	t	s
d	c	l
r	sh	h

MEMORY TRAINING

- Say each list of words three times.
- How many can you remember?
- Write them in your notebook. Check.
- Write your scores here.

....

3 Name the pictures.

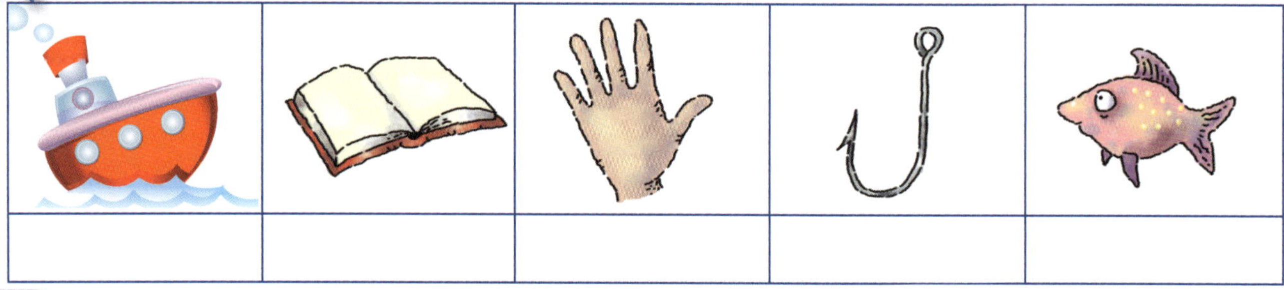

TARGETING SPELLING 1 © PASCAL PRESS ISBN 9781925490190

RULE

Add **-es** to **nouns** ending in **sh** and **ch** to make them **plural**. *Example: dish, **dishes***

4 Write these nouns in *plural* form (more than one).

dish ____________ fox ____________ bus ____________

boss ____________ rich ____________ box ____________

5 Add a *vowel* to make some criss-cross words.

	ch	
sh	i	p
	n	

	ch	
sh		d
	ck	

	f	
r		ch
	sh	

	ch	
d		sh
	ll	

	m	
ch		t
	sh	

Verbs are *doing words*. Add **-s** or **-es** if they follow the words ***she***, ***he*** or ***it***. *Examples: Jill (**She**) **shuts** the door. Bill (**He**) **fishes** in the creek. The duck (**It**) **swims** in the pond.*

6 Add -s or -es to complete the *verbs*.

Remember, we add -es to words ending in s, x, sh and ch.

Water **gush**_____ from the garden tap.

Tom **toss**_____ the ball to Kai and he **kick**_____ it.

Jason **wish**_____ he had a pet dog.

Dan **get**_____ a bucket and **fill**_____ it with water.

She **look**_____ out the window and **see**_____ a magpie.

Billy **go**_____ outside and **play**_____ with his dog.

UNIT 8 Letter Teams: th

th has two sounds — a *buzzing* sound that you hear in the words ***this***, ***that*** and ***they***; and a *blowing* sound that you hear in the words ***thing***, ***think*** and ***thump***.

SEE & SAY

this	**with**
that	**moth**
them	**path**

for

one

two

1 Write the word for each picture.

This is my pet  . ____________

These are my 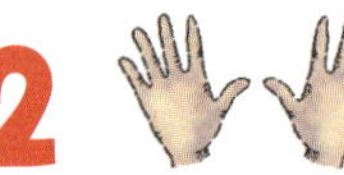 . 

That is my pet  . 

Those are my red  . ____________

Pronouns *take the place of* **nouns**.
They, ***them*** and ***their*** are pronouns.
Examples: ***They*** *(The boys) rode* ***their*** *(the boys') bikes to the park.* ***They*** *(The boys) rode* ***them*** *(the bikes) along the path.*

2 Choose from they, them or their to complete the sentences.

The children came inside after __________ ball game.

Mum told __________ to wash __________ hands.

Then she gave __________ some cakes to eat.

__________ all said, "Thank you."

TARGETING SPELLING 1 © PASCAL PRESS ISBN 9781925490190

A **compound word** is made up of *two words*.
Examples: ***pig*** + ***pen*** = ***pigpen***; ***sun*** + ***set*** = ***sunset***

3 Put a line between each word in these *compound words*.

Examples: **pig|pen sun|set**

hilltop bedroom lipstick bathtub

popcorn bathroom footpath chopsticks

WORD TRAPS

Don't mix up **four** (4) and **for**.
Examples: I saw ***four*** *(4) hens and* ***four*** *(4) ducks.*
This book is ***for*** *you. I went* ***for*** *a swim.*

Don't mix up **two** (2) and **to**.
Examples: I have ***two*** *legs and* ***two*** *arms.*
We go ***to*** *school. I went* ***to*** *the shop. Go* ***to*** *sleep.*

4 Write the missing words.

This is a ________. That is a ________.

This is a ______________. That is a top ________.

2 This is ________. 4 That is ________.

These are ________. Those are ________.

5 Write these nouns in *plural* form (more than one).

moth ________ peg ________ fox ________

path ________ pup ________ bus ________

TARGETING SPELLING 1 © PASCAL PRESS ISBN 9781925490190

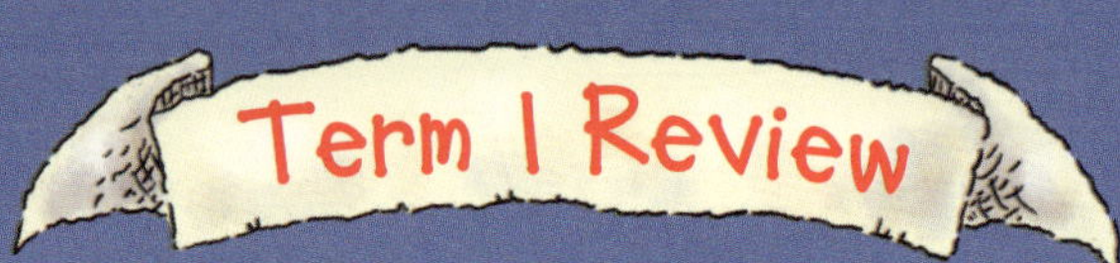

1 Name the pictures.

2 Write these nouns in *plural* form.

log ________ bus ________ rock ________

box ________ bag ________ pet ________

hill ________ chip ________ man ________

3 Add an ending to the words in bold. Choose from -s and -es.

Katy **wish**___ she had a ball to play with.

Mum **chop**___ the apples and **cook**___ them in a pot.

Dan **get**___ the ball and **run**___ to the line.

Eli **go**___ to the window and **look**___ outside.

Tom **shut**___ the door and **toss**___ his hat on the bed.

4 Complete these sentences.

It's ____.

I'm ____.

TARGETING SPELLING 1 © PASCAL PRESS ISBN 9781925490190

Term 1 Review

5 Write words of *opposite* meaning (e.g. *long, short*).

happy ________ cold ________ dry ________

thick ________ little ________ stop ________

down ________ out ________ fat ________

Add a *pronoun* from the box to complete each sentence.

I	my	me	he	she	we

Ben said, "_____ have lost _____ ball."

_____ friend Gabby gave _____ a box of chocolates.

_____ like to ride our bikes in the park.

Bella said that _____ would lend _____ her pencil.

Join the words to make *compound words*.

bed	corn	foot	top
bath	room	sun	sticks
back	stick	chop	bag
pop	tub	hill	path
lip	pack	hand	set

Colour the correct word in the brackets.

Katy [look looks] for a gift [four for] her mum.

The boys went [to two] the shop [four for] milk.

Jack [go goes] to school with his [for four] best friends.

They had [fan fun] kicking balls into the [net nut].

Consonant Blends: br, gr

Many words begin with **br**, as in ***brick*** and ***brush***.
Many words begin with **gr**, as in ***grab*** and ***grip***.
Note how we blend the two consonant sounds together when we say these words.

SEE & SAY

brat	**grip**
brush	**grab**
brick	**grub**

in
her
him

1 **Write the *two letters* that begin each picture.**

Pronouns take the place of **nouns**.
Her and ***him*** are pronouns. Write ***her*** for girls and ***him*** for boys.
*Examples: I gave **her** a ribbon for **her** hair. I gave **him** a football.*

TARGETING SPELLING 1 © PASCAL PRESS ISBN 9781925490190

UNIT 9

2 Add the missing *pronoun*. Choose from her, him or them.

Katy gave ________ friend a bunch of flowers.

Ben has a football. His dad gave it to ________.

Mum cut some roses and put ________ in a vase.

Jade asked me to play with ________ after school.

3 Run your finger down the *letter slide*. Write the word under each slide.

br	*br*	*br*	*br*
i	*u*	*a*	*i*
ck	*sh*	*g*	*m*
brick	________	________	________

gr	*gr*	*gr*	*gr*
a	*i*	*i*	*u*
n	*p*	*ll*	*ff*
________	________	________	________

4 Write these nouns in *plural* form by adding -s or -es.

brick ________ brush ________ moth ________

grub ________ chick ________ dish ________

5 Write a sentence about a *grasshopper*.

____.

6 Unscramble this sentence. Start with the word in **bold**.

teeth go **Brush** and to your bed.

____.

7 Unscramble these animals. Start with the letter in **bold**.

ta**c** **d**go i**p**g ukc**d** e**h**n

________ ________ ________ ________ ________

Consonant Blends: fr, dr

Many words begin with fr, as in *frog* and *fresh*.
Many words begin with dr, as in *drop* and *drum*.
Note how we blend the two consonant sounds together when we say these words.

SEE & SAY

frog	drip
from	drop
fresh	drum

us
up
be

1 Choose a word from the *See and Say* list to complete the sentences.

I like ________ bread with butter and jam.

Andy hits his toy ________ with two sticks.

Do not ________ the eggs!

The green ________ hopped into the pond.

2 Write the *consonant blend* that begins each picture.

3 Colour the correct *pronoun* in the brackets.

The teacher told [we us] to open our books.

[They Them] are going to swim in the pool.

Sophie was hungry, so Mum gave [she her] an apple.

[Him He] went to play with [him his] friends.

TARGETING SPELLING 1 © PASCAL PRESS ISBN 9781925490190

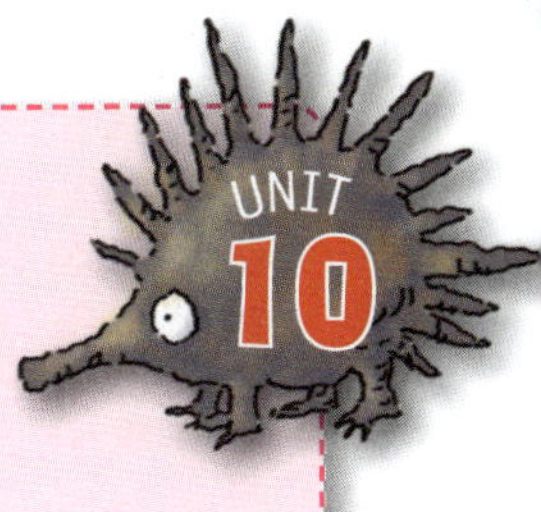

Some words *describe* **nouns**. They say more about them.
These words are called **adjectives**.

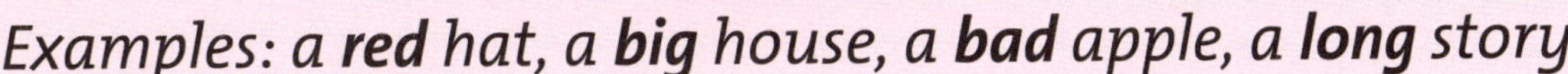
*Examples: a **red** hat, a **big** house, a **bad** apple, a **long** story*

4 **Write a *noun* beside each adjective.** *Example: a tall **tree***

a fat ________________ a hot ________________

a pink ________________ a sad ________________

wet ________________ fresh ________________

The letter **y** can be added to nouns to make **adjectives**.
*Examples: bush**y**, wind**y**, lump**y***

5 **Build *adjectives* by adding -y to these nouns.**

hill ________________ luck ________________

dress ________________ frill ________________

trick ________________ rock ________________

hand ________________ chill ________________

6 **Write these nouns in *plural* form by adding -s or -es.**

frog ________________ dress ________________

wish ________________ frill ________________

drum ________________ moth ________________

7 **Colour the correct word in the brackets.**

Water [grips drips] from the garden tap.

Dad will [drill grill] a hole in the wall.

I saw a [grab grub] under the green leaf.

Did you see the green tree [frog from]?

UNIT 11

Consonant Blends: pr, tr, cr

Many words begin with **pr** (*pram*), **tr** (*truck*) and **cr** (*crab*). Note how we blend the two sounds together.

pr
tr
cr

SEE & SAY

pram	press
trap	truck
crab	cross

LOOK & LEARN

three
as
you

Choose a word from the *See and Say* list to complete the sentences.

The baby is asleep in the _________.

I saw a _________ on the sand.

Dad drives a big red _________.

Look both ways before you _________ the street.

Mum will _________ my clothes for school.

2 Write the *consonant blend* that begins each picture.

				he, she, we, they

Write the *rhyming words*. Read them three times.

pram	press	track	crab
cr____	dr____	cr____	gr____
gr____	m____	sh____	dr____

MEMORY TRAINING

In your notebook, write the words you can remember. Check. Write your score here.

....

TARGETING SPELLING 1 © PASCAL PRESS ISBN 9781925490190

Run your finger down the *letter slide*.
Write the word under each slide.

pr i ck	pr o p	cr o p	cr a sh
prick	________	________	________

tr a ck	tr i ck	tr i p	tr a m
________	________	________	________

Write these nouns in *plural* form.

trap ________ crab ________ pram ________

truck ________ crop ________ brush ________

Write each *number* as a word.

1 ________ 2 ________ 3 ________ 4 ________

Colour the pairs of words that are *opposite* in meaning.
Use a different colour for each pair.

open	up	yes	out	cold	top
bottom	no	hot	shut	down	in

Unscramble this sentence. Start with the word in **bold**.

crab into **The** wet the sand. dug

____.

TARGETING SPELLING 1 © PASCAL PRESS ISBN 9781925490190

Consonant Blends: pl, fl

Many words begin with pl, as in ***plum*** and ***plug***. Many words begin with fl, as in ***flap*** and ***flag***. Note how we blend the two consonant sounds together when we say these words.

pl
fl

SEE & SAY

plan	flat
plum	flag
plug	flap

LOOK & LEARN

are
play
four

Write the *consonant blend* that begins each picture.

The words **is** and **are** are verbs. The verb **is** follows one noun or pronoun. *Examples: Jill* ***is*** *sleepy. She* ***is*** *going to bed.*
The verb **are** follows a plural noun or pronoun. *Examples: The boys* ***are*** *in the playground. They* ***are*** *playing football.*

Choose is or are to complete each sentence.

The man _____ in the big red truck.

There _____ flags flapping in the wind.

A plum _____ a sweet red fruit.

The boxes _____ full of toys.

TARGETING SPELLING 1 © PASCAL PRESS ISBN 9781925490190

Run your finger down the *letter slide*. Write the word under each slide.

pl o t — plot

pl o d — ______

pl o p — ______

pl u ck — ______

fl u ff — ______

fl o p — ______

fl o ck — ______

fl a sh — ______

4 Add the *missing consonant blend*. Choose from pl or fl.

I saw a ____**ock** of seagulls flying over the sea.

There are ____**ants** growing in my garden.

Put the ____**ug** in the sink.

My bike has a ____**at** tyre.

Will you come and ____**ay** ball with me?

5 Write the *rhyming words*. Read them three times.

pl**um**	fl**at**	fl**ap**	fl**ag**
dr____	br____	tr____	dr____
ch____	ch____	ch____	br____

MEMORY TRAINING

In your notebook, write the words you can remember. Check. Write your score here.

....

Write these nouns in *plural* form.

plum ____________	flag ____________	plug ____________
cross ____________	truck ____________	dress ____________

Consonant Blends: bl, gl

Many words begin with **bl**, as in ***bl**ack* and ***bl**ock*.
Many words begin with **gl**, as in ***gl**ad* and ***gl**um*.
Note how we blend the two consonant sounds together when we say these words.

SEE & SAY

bled	glad
black	glum
block	glass

LOOK & LEARN

went
so
five

Choose a word from the *See and Say* list to complete the sentences.

I am __________ you can come to my party.

The little girl drank a __________ of milk.

Bella has __________ hair.

Dad gave me a __________ of chocolate.

Verbs show *when* things happen — NOW or in the PAST.

*We **go** to school. (NOW)* — *We **went** to school. (PAST)*

*John **runs** to school. (NOW)* — *John **ran** to school. (PAST)*

2 **Match the now verbs and the past verbs.**

Now	Past	Now	Past
go	saw	do	sat
see	went	sit	was
run	got	dig	did
get	ran	is	dug

TARGETING SPELLING 1 © PASCAL PRESS ISBN 9781925490190

Write the word for each picture.

I had a  of fizzy lemonade. __________

A  ran after the . __________ __________

I  my hair and put on my . __________ __________

The  has a load of . __________ __________

Add the missing *consonant blend*. Choose from bl, gl, pl or fl.

The chicks are soft and ___**uffy**.

I had a ___**um** and a ___**ass** of milk.

The ___**ag** will ___**ap** in the wind.

Kai likes to ___**ay** with his ___**ocks**.

Mend the broken words by adding a *vowel* (a, e, i, o, u).

Tom **h**__**t** the ball with his **b**__**t**.

Sam wore **bl**__**ck** shoes and white **s**__**cks**.

We **r**__**n** to see the **d**__**cks** on the pond.

Joe **br**__**shed** his teeth and went to **b**__**d**.

Jimmy **h**__**t** his **dr**__**m** with two **st**__**cks**.

Write the *rhyming words*. Read them three times.

gl**um**	gl**ass**	bl**ock**
dr___	gr___	fl___
pl___	cl___	fr___

MEMORY TRAINING

In your notebook, write the words you can remember. Check. Write your score here.

....

Write each *number* as a word.

1__________ 2__________ 3__________ 4__________ 5__________

Consonant Blends: sl, cl

Many words begin with sl, as in *slam* and *slap*.
Many words begin with cl, as in *clap* and *clock*.
Note how we blend the two consonant sounds together when we say these words.

SEE & SAY

slam	clap
slap	clip
slip	clock

if
have
by

1 Choose a word from the *See and Say* list to complete the sentences.

I can hear a ________ ticking.

________ your hands three times.

Don't ________ in the wet mud.

Don't ________ the door!

2 Write the *consonant blend* that begins each picture.

TARGETING SPELLING 1 © PASCAL PRESS ISBN 9781925490190

3 Write these nouns in *plural* form.

clock ____________ glass ____________ block ____________

bus ____________ brick ____________ class ____________

4 Run your finger down the *letter slide*. Write the word under each slide.

sl o t	sl e d	sl i m	sl a sh
slot	____________	____________	____________

cl u b	cl o g	cl i ck	cl a sh
____________	____________	____________	____________

5 Make a wall of *rhyming words*. Read them three times.

slip	tr___	gr___	dr___
fl___	sh___	cl___	sk___

MEMORY TRAINING

In your notebook, write the words you can remember. Check. Write your score here.

....

6 Write an ending for these sentences.

I have ____.

If I could fly, I ____

____.

7 Join the *consonant blend* to the stem to write these words.

cl — og ____________
cl — am ____________
cl — uck ____________

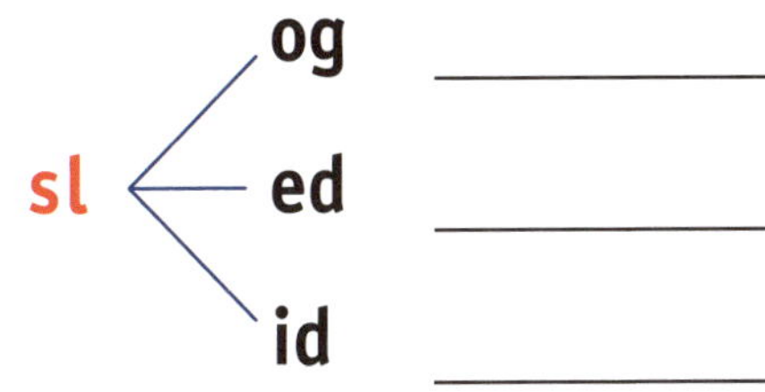

sl — og ____________
sl — ed ____________
sl — id ____________

TARGETING SPELLING 1 © PASCAL PRESS ISBN 9781925490190

Consonant Blends: st, sm

Many words begin with **st**, as in ***stop*** and ***stick***.
Many words begin with **sm**, as in ***smell*** and ***smack***.
Note how we blend the two consonant sounds together when we say these words.

SEE & SAY

stop	smell
step	small
stick	smack

six
come
do

1 **Choose a word from the *See and Say* list to complete the sentences.**

The car will ________ at the red light.

A ________ mouse ran under the bed.

I can ________ dinner cooking.

I toss a ________ and my dog runs after it.

Write these nouns in *plural* form.

stick ________ step ________

class ________ smell ________

Read the words three times, In your notebook, write the words you can remember. Check. Write your scores here.

....

Write the rhyming words from the *word wheel* and on the *word ladder*.

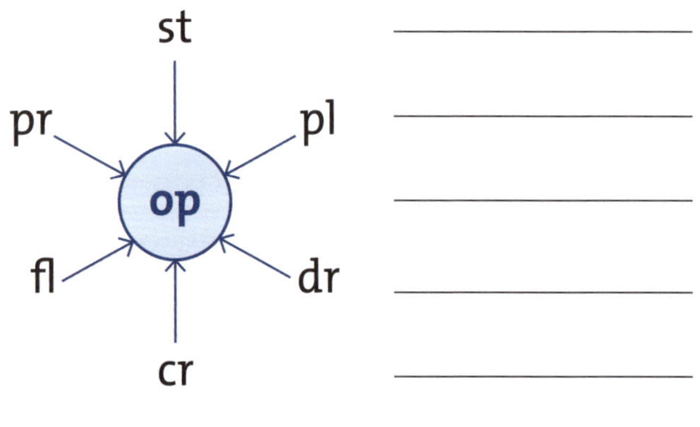

____
____
____
____
____
____

back
r
p
st

sm
bl
tr
sh

TARGETING SPELLING 1 © PASCAL PRESS ISBN 9781925490190

4 Colour the correct word in the brackets.

My friend has [block black] hair.

The truck got [stick stuck] in the mud.

Come and [smell small] the roses in my garden.

Dad will [step stop] at the school gate to let me off.

5 Make a wall of *rhyming words*. Read them three times.

mash tr____ cr____ fl____

sm____ sl____ cl____

MEMORY TRAINING

In your notebook, write the words you can remember. Check. Write your score here. ....

REVIEW

Verbs are *doing words*. Add -s or -es if they follow the words ***she***, ***he*** or ***it***. *Examples: Jill (**She**) **shuts** the door. Bill (**He**) **fishes** in the creek. The duck (**It**) **swims** in the pond.*

6 Complete this table of *verbs*.

I run	*You run*	*He runs*
We clap	They clap	She
You sit	We sit	It
I dress	You dress	She
I wish	They wish	He

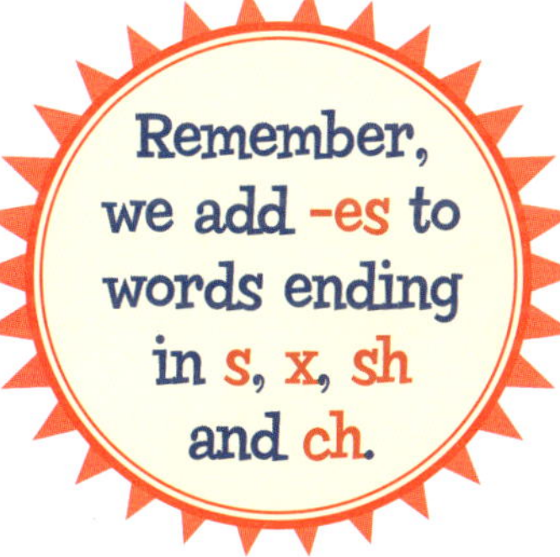

7 Name the pictures.

Consonant Blends: sp, sn

Many words begin with sp, as in ***spot*** and ***spell***.
Many words begin with sn, as in ***snap*** and ***sniff***.
Note how we blend the two consonant sounds together when we say these words.

SEE & SAY

spot	sniff
spin	snap
spit	snack

LOOK & LEARN

his
off
not

1. Write the *consonant blend* that begins each picture.

2. Write these nouns in *plural* form.

spot ______	snack ______	drum ______
brush ______	glass ______	trap ______
track ______	flag ______	speck ______

3. Colour the pairs of words that are *opposite* in meaning. Use a different colour for each pair.

shut	up	sit	on	small	back
big	off	down	open	front	stand

TARGETING SPELLING 1 © PASCAL PRESS ISBN 9781925490190

4 Add a *vowel* to mend the broken words. (a, e, i, o, u).

Zoe wore a **r__d dr__ss** with white **sp__ts**.

Round and round **sp__ns** the small **t__p**.

We have a small **sn__ck** at 11 **o'cl__ck**.

Kayla likes **f__sh** and **ch__ps** for **l__nch**.

5 Make a wall of *rhyming words*. Read them three times.

hot	n___	tr___	sp___
sl___	pl___	bl___	sh___

MEMORY TRAINING

In your notebook, write the words you can remember. Check. Write your score here.

....

6 Colour the correct *consonant blend*.

Cl / Sl **ap** your hands and cr / st **amp** your feet.

I can tr / sn **ap** this little tr / st **ick** in two.

My dog pl / tr **ots** behind my dad's tr / pl **uck**.

Don't sp / gr **ill** the milk and don't cr / dr **op** the eggs.

7 Draw some funny pictures.

A frog with red spots	The best snack of all time!	My smelly socks!	A big ant playing the drums

Term 2 Review

1 Name the pictures.

2 Write each of these nouns in *plural* form.

plum	____________	cross	____________	truck	____________
clock	____________	plan	____________	brush	____________
glass	____________	spot	____________	dress	____________

3 For each word, write the word of *opposite* meaning.

open	____________	cold	____________	dry	____________
out	____________	big	____________	on	____________
down	____________	go	____________	happy	____________

4 Colour the correct *pronoun* in the brackets.

Karen comes to school with [her you] sister.

[I Me] have three hot buns for [they them].

Do [them you] want to play ball with [me he]?

[We Him] asked Dad to take [us she] to the beach.

[They Them] came to the park to walk [them their] dogs.

TARGETING SPELLING 1 © PASCAL PRESS ISBN 9781925490190

Unit 1

1 cat, hat, man, can
2 cap, cow, clown, cup; ball, boat, bone, box; mouse, mug, moon
3 handwriting practice
4 memory training: cat, fat, bat, mat, rat; man, pan, fan, tan, van
5 fan, mat, van, pan, bat

Unit 2

1 red, fed, pet, get, bed, let
2 wet, set, net, vet, met, jet; men, ten, hen, pen, then, den
3 handwriting practice
4 hat, pet, hen, bat, net, bed
5 hens, bells, bags, fans, beds, legs
6 can, shells, sand; hens, pen, fed; dress, red, hat

Unit 3

1 fill, Did, hill, Will, lid, hid
2 memory training: pin, bin, fin, tin, win; hit, bit, fit, sit, kit; pig, big, fig, dig, wig
3 handwriting practice
4 pig, lips, bin, bib, zip
5 pins, pigs, bins, pegs, pets, beds, cats, vans, bags
6 hat, lid, bed, hill, man, shell
7 writing activity

Unit 4

1 got, dog, fog, dog, log, not, hot
2 memory training: pot, cot, lot, shot, dot, rot
3 top, hop; rod, nod; box, fox; jog, bog; toss, boss
4 handwriting practice
5 doll, bed, zip, fan, bat, hen, dog, pig
6 logs, foxes, dolls, pots, bosses
7 cold–hot; happy–sad; little–big; dry–wet; thin–thick; good–bad

Unit 5

1 fun, sun, run, cut, nuts
2 memory training: bug, tug, rug, mug, pug, dug, hug, jug
3 bug, sum, jug, bus, mug, sun
4 handwriting practice
5 tub, cub, rub; hum, gum, mum; mud, cud, bud; rut, jut, hut; sun, bun, gun
6 She, He, me, me
7 tub, bell, hat, pig, fox
8 cups, nuts, mugs, buns, cubs

Unit 6

1 six, ducks, socks, sun, sack, dog
2 memory training: kick, tick, lick, pick, sick, wick, quick
3 ducks, hands, rats, nuts, hills, rocks
4 lock, neck, socks, ducks, quack, quack
5 rock, pack, kick, pick
6 peck, buck, dock, suck

TARGETING SPELLING 1 © PASCAL PRESS ISBN 9781925490190

Unit 7

1 Examples: shop, shot, shock, shod; fish, fit, fin, fill, fig; chip, chin, chill, chick; much, mum, mud, muck, mug
2 memory training: mash, lash, cash, dash, rash; look, book, took, cook, shook; and, band, sand, land, hand
3 ship, book, hand, hook, fish
4 dishes, bosses, foxes, riches, buses, boxes
5 check, shed; fish, rich; chill, dish; mash, chat
6 gushes, tosses, kicks, wishes, gets, fills, looks, sees, goes, plays

Unit 8

1 dog, two, hands, cat, socks
2 The children came inside after **their** ball game. Mum told **them** to wash **their** hands. Then she gave **them** some cakes to eat. **They** all said, "Thank you."
3 hill top; pop corn; bed room; bath room; lip stick; foot path; bath tub; chop sticks
4 fish, moth, two, hens, pig, hat, four, ducks
5 moths, paths, pegs, pups, foxes, buses

Term 1 review

1 cat, dog, fish, hen, duck, pig, sun, socks, bed, man
2 logs, boxes, hills, buses, bags, chips, rocks, pets, men
3 wishes, chops, cooks, gets, runs, goes, looks, shuts, tosses
4 writing activity
5 happy-sad; thick-thin; down-up; cold-hot; little-big; out-in; dry-wet; stop-go; fat-thin
6 I, my; My, me; We; she, me
7 bathtub, backpack, popcorn, lipstick, footpath, sunset, chopsticks, hilltop, handbag
8 looks, for; to, for; goes, four; fun, net

Unit 9

1 br, gr, br, sh, gr, th, br, ch, br, sh
2 her, him, them, her
3 blending activity: brick, brush, brag, brim, gran, grip, grill, gruff
4 bricks, grubs, brushes, chicks, moths, dishes
5 writing activity
6 Brush your teeth and go to bed.
7 cat, dog. pig, duck, hen

Unit 10

1 fresh, drum, drop, frog
2 dr, fr, dr, fr, dr
3 us, They, her, He, his
4 answers will vary
5 hilly, dressy, tricky, handy, lucky, frilly, rocky, chilly
6 frogs, wishes, drums, dresses, frills, moths
7 drips, drill, grub, frog

TARGETING SPELLING 1 © PASCAL PRESS ISBN 9781925490190

Unit 11

1 pram, crab, truck, cross, press
2 cr, tr, pr, tr, cr, pr, cr, tr, cr, pr
3 memory training: pram, cram, gram; press, dress, mess; track, crack, shack; crab, grab, drab
4 blending activity: prick, prop, crop, crash, track, trick, trip, tram
5 traps, trucks, crabs, crops, prams, brushes
6 one, two, three, four
7 open-shut; up-down; yes-no; out-in; cold-hot; top-bottom
8 The crab dug into the wet sand.

Unit 12

1 pl, fl, pl, tr, dr, fl, pr, pl, cr, fl
2 is, are, is, are
3 blending activity: plot, plod, plop, pluck, fluff, flop, flock, flash
4 flock, plants, plug, flat, play
5 memory training: plum, drum, chum; flat, brat, chat; flap, trap, chap; flag, drag, brag
6 plums, crosses, flags, trucks, plugs, dresses

Unit 13

1 glad, glass, black, block
2 see-saw; run-ran; get-got; do-did; sit-sat; dig-dug; is-was
3 glass, fox, hens, brush, socks, truck, bricks
4 fluffy, plum, glass, flag, flap, play, blocks
5 hit, bat, black, socks, ran, ducks, brushed, bed, hit, drum, sticks
6 memory training: glum, drum, plum; glass, grass, class; block, flock, frock
7 one, two, three, four, five

Unit 14

1 clock, Clap, slip, slam
2 cl, gl, sl, cl, tr, cl, sl, cl, pr, sl
3 clocks, buses, glasses, bricks, blocks, classes
4 blending activity: slot, sled, slim, slash, club, clog, click, clash
5 memory training: slip, trip, grip, drip, flip, ship, clip, skip
6 writing activity
7 clog, clam, cluck; slog, sled, slid

Unit 15

1 stop, small, smell, stick
2 sticks, classes, steps, smells
3 memory training: word ladder: back, rack, pack, stack, smack, black, track, shack
word wheel: stop, plop, drop, crop, flop, prop
4 black, stuck, smell, stop
5 memory training: mash, trash, crash, flash, smash, slash, clash
6 claps, sits, dresses, wishes
7 clock, pram, stop, truck, frog, blocks, glasses, flag, stick, crab

Unit 16

1 sp, sn, st, sp, br, sn, dr, cr, sn, sp
2 spots, brushes, tracks, snacks, glasses, flags, drums, traps, specks
3 shut-open; up-down; sit-stand; on-off; small-big; back-front
4 red, dress, spots, spins, top, snack, o'clock, fish, chips, lunch
5 memory training: hot, not, trot, spot, slot, plot, blot, shot
6 clap, stamp, snap, stick, trots, truck, spill, drop
7 Drawing activity

TARGETING SPELLING 1 © PASCAL PRESS ISBN 9781925490190

Term 2 review

1 drum, stick, pram, plug, blocks, frog, glass, flag, clock, crab

2 plums, clocks, glasses, crosses, plans, spots, trucks, brushes, dresses

3 open-shut (close); out-in; down-up; cold-hot; big-small (little); go-stop (come); dry-wet; on-off; happy-sad

4 her; I, them; you, me; We, us; They, their

5 chilly, messy, tricky, smelly, fluffy, glossy

6 does, looks, crosses, flaps, takes, presses, claps

7 drips, Step, small, flag, stop, glass, bun

8 do-did; dig-dug; sit-sat; go-went; see-saw; get-got; is-was

9 one, two, three, four, five, six

Unit 17

1 foxes, sticks, bosses, crosses, pluses, bricks, taxes, flags, brushes

2 presses, comes, snaps, grabs, tosses, dresses, packs

3 memory training: toss, moss, boss, gloss, cross; mess, dress, press, less, bless

4 are, was, am, was, were

5 kissing, pressing, tossing, crossing, missing, dressing

6 is (was), were, are (were), am (was), are (were)

Unit 18

1 wall, tall, hall, small, stall, fall; bell, tell, sell, shell, spell, yell

2 calling, friends, tosses, balls, falling, trees, clocks, ticking

3 memory training: will, fill, grill, hill, still, mill, drill, kill, spill, chill

4 hilly, lucky, glossy, smelly, messy, rocky, bossy, sticky, sandy

5 were, are, are (were), is, am

6 isn't, weren't, wasn't, aren't

Unit 19

1 past, last, west, best

2 nesting, trees, tossing, crusts, ducks, misty, chilly, resting, swims

3 here-there; west-east; fast-slow; tall-short; lost-found; first-last

4 blending activity: list, twist, lost, cost

5 memory training: nest, pest, rest, chest, vest, quest; dust, gust, rust, must, just, crust

6 spilled, smelled, rested, kicked, twisted, crushed

7 dusty, gusty, frosty, misty, rusty, crusty

TARGETING SPELLING 1 © PASCAL PRESS ISBN 9781925490190

Unit 20

1 hang, sing, wings, rang
2 memory training: ring, king, thing, swing, sting, bring, cling, sling, string, spring
3 ringing, swings, hits, swishes, tosses, bringing, falls, clings
4 rings, strings, things, fangs, wings, kings
5 ring-rang; come-came; go-went; do-did; sting-stung; sell-sold; hang-hung
6 crashed, tree, trots, track, trucks, stop, cross, step, crabs
7 hung (hangs), wings, sang, fast

Unit 21

1 stung, along, long, hung
2 Examples: sing, wing, king, ring, sting; hang, sang, rang, fang, bang, gang; song, long, dong, thong; hung, sung, rung, stung, swung, clung
3 one, two, three, four, five, six, seven, eight
4 swung, sang, ring, hung, sting
5 swinging, sings, dances, plays, bumped, spilled, dresses, makes, bringing
6 long-short; good-bad; small-big; buy-sell; stop-go; in-out
7 Jess saw a plane flying in the sky.

Unit 22

1 band, lend, mend, sand
2 hands, songs, things, ponds, classes, brands
3 handy, sandy, windy, glossy, misty, smelly, rocky, hilly, tricky
4 blending activity: hand, land, stand, brand, bend, spend, pond, fond
5 mending, handed, dressed, brushed, playing, singing
6 send-sent; lend-lent; spend-spent; give-gave; come-came; stand-stood; make-made
7 They, their, His, him, She, me, We, them

Unit 23

1 tent, plant, went, ant
2 ant, ring, tent, king, plant, ball, clock, swing, fish, bell
3 blending activity: grant, slant, spent, vent, dint, hint, blunt, grunt
4 memory training: nine, mine, shine, dine, fine, line, pine, vine, wine, spine
5 sprinted, planting, grunting, rolling, puffed, panted, glinting
6 hill side; wind mill; grand mother; foot ball; hat band; grand stand; song bird; sand hill
7 writing activity

TARGETING SPELLING 1 © PASCAL PRESS ISBN 9781925490190

Unit 24

1 drank, bank, blink, sink
2 thanked, sinking, filled, tanks, thinking, missing
3 stink-stank; drink-drank; think-thought; go-went; buy-bought; take-took; is-was
4 blending activity: tank, yank, trunk, chunk, wink, stink, think, drink
5 trunk, drank, long, bunk, beds, crackers, chunk, sank, rocks
6 junk yard; home work; grand father; sand bank; net ball; take away; river bank; hair brush
7 writing activity

Term 3 review

1 ball, spots, swing, ant, ring, nest, tent, shell, hand, bell
2 bands, songs, dishes, wings, crosses, dolls, tests, things, glasses
3 calls, calling, called; presses, pressing, pressed; thanks, thanking, thanked; twists, twisting, twisted
4 one, two, three, four, five, six, seven, eight, nine, ten
5 sing-sang; go-went; send-sent; do-did; give-gave; is-was
6 slow-fast (quick); here-there; first-last; bad-good; short-tall (long); on-off
7 mending, holes, socks, planted, trees, bushes, playing, sandy, kicks (kicked), tosses (tossed); frosty, chilly
8 windmill, homework, football, junkyard, netball, sandhill, grandstand
9 rang, their, hung, eight

Unit 25

1 jump, ramp, stump, damp, lamp
2 lamp, camp, scamp, clamp, stamp, tramp; bump, dump, hump, pump, slump, clump
3 bumpy, chunky, lumpy, grumpy
4 tramping, jumped, pumps (pumped), fills (filled), bumped, camping
5 come-came; give-gave; see-saw; sing-sang; go-went
6 lamp, humps, thump, Drink, bump, dump, clump, stamp
You are a champion.

Unit 26

1 lift, stiff, left, soft
2 memory training: lift, gift, shift, drift, swift; stuff, puff, muff, cuff, fluff
3 small, left, long, soft
4 longer, longest; quicker, quickest; colder, coldest; smaller, smallest
5 drifting, puffing, panting, lifted, fluffy, opened, gifts
6 lift, stuff, shift, muff
7 writing activity

Unit 27

1 witch, match, pitch, patch
2 memory training: catch, batch, latch, snatch, scratch, hatch
3 keep, sheep, deep, jeep, sleep, peep, weep, steep, creep, beep
4 crutches, catches, Fridays, clutching, hands, hatched, matches
5 itchy, patchy, fluffy, scruffy, bumpy, grumpy
6 word search
7 pitch, scratch, which, hatch, Catch

TARGETING SPELLING 1 © PASCAL PRESS ISBN 9781925490190

Unit 28

1 bunches, punches, benches, lunches, branches, finches
2 memory training: day, say, pay, may, lay, hay, bay, way, play, sway, stay, tray
3 drawing activity
4 bunch, pitch, bench, crutches
5 punching, benches, lunches, clenched (clenches), crunchy, scrunched, tossed
6 boxer, jumper, hunter, speller, farmer

Unit 29

1 shelf, mask, task, wisps
2 bench, mask, golf, shelf, lamp
3 two, three, four, seven, eight, nine
4 crunching, asked, paintbrushes, walking, wisps, trees, played, balls
5 over-under; little-big; boy-girl; day-night; here-there; left-right
6 herself, yourself, myself, itself, himself
7 masks, flasks, tasks, desks, risks, baskets

Unit 30

1 grubs; dresses; fills; jumps; benches; balls; claps; smashes; blocks; foxes; munches; kisses
2 missing, drinking; tested, bumped; smelly, risky; sinker, stinger; longest, richest
3 Yes: trot, rip, cut, skip, drop, swim, grab

   No: camp, long, trick, press, pump
4 running, packing, skipping, cutting; stopped, crashed, tripped, jumped; muddy, lucky, frosty, sunny; richer, wetter, thinner, softer; longest, fattest, saddest, slimmest

Unit 31

1 tight, might, right, high
2 memory training: might, night, tight, light, fight, fright, sight, slight, right, bright
3 lighter, lightest; brighter, brightest; tighter, tightest
4 fight, witch, light, night, mask
5 bright-dull; light-heavy; right-wrong; dark-light; night-day; tight-loose
6 packing, running, lifting, hopping, crashing, slipped, tramped, hummed, filled, spotted, funny, lumpy, muddy, tricky, baggy, thinner, thinnest; wetter, wettest; bigger, biggest; longer, longest; fatter, fattest

Unit 32

1 memory training: art, cart, dart, smart, start, chart; park, mark, dark, shark, bark, spark
2 cars, stars, parks, carts, sharks, jars, yards, arms, cards
3 car, shark, barn, star, jar
4 marked, handed, darting, started, barking, running, jumped, skipped
5 artwork, parkland, highway, moonlight, nightdress, farmyard
6 smarter, sharpest (sharper), darker, stronger, hardest
7 writing activity

Term 4 Review

1 star, mask, swing, hand, fight, golf, bench, shark, light, tent
2 tasks, stitches, gifts, lunches, lamps, boxes, pumps, days, classes
3 pumps, pumping, pumped; hops, hopping, hopped; flashes, flashing, flashed; pats, patting, patted
4 one, two, three, four, five, six, seven, eight, nine, ten
5 baggy, misty, foggy, frosty, muddy, skinny, funny, crunchy, fluffy
6 give-gave; run-ran; get-got; go-went; do-did; see-saw; fall-fell; sit-sat
7 big-little (small); over-under; first-last; left-right; low-high; hard-soft; short-long; day-night; slow-fast (quick)
8 skipping, taller, sunny, jumped
9 bookmark, lunchbox, highway, moonlight, farmyard, haystack, bookshelf

TARGETING SPELLING 1 © PASCAL PRESS ISBN 9781925490190

5 Build *adjectives* by adding -y to these nouns.

chill ________ trick ________ fluff ________

mess ________ smell ________ gloss ________

6 Add -s or -es to complete each *verb*.

Jake **do**___ not like plums or nuts.

Jim **look**___ both ways before he **cross**___ the street.

A bird **flap**___ its wings as it **take**___ off.

Jill **press**___ the doorbell three times.

The baby **clap**___ its little hands.

7 Circle the correct word in the brackets.

Water [grips drips] from the tap.

[Stop Step] up onto this [small smell] box.

He held up a red [drag flag] to [stop drop] the car.

I had a [class glass] of milk and a sticky [bin bun].

8 Match the now verbs and the past verbs.

Now	Past	Now	Past
run	dug	go	saw
do	sat	see	went
dig	ran	get	was
sit	did	is	got

9 Write each *number* as a word.

1 ________ 2 ________ 3 ________

4 ________ 5 ________ 6 ________

Word Endings: -ss

Some words end in -ss. If they are nouns, add -es to make them plural. *Example*: *kiss, kisses*.
If they are verbs, add -es when they follow *he*, *she* or *it*.
Examples: *I toss, he tosses; I kiss, she kisses*

SEE & SAY

toss	miss
loss	less
boss	press

seven
goes
going

1 Write each noun in *plural* form.

fox	________	cross	________	tax	________
stick	________	plus	________	flag	________
boss	________	brick	________	brush	________

2 Add -s or -es to the *verbs* in bold.

David **press**___ the doorbell.

Jim's dog **come**___ when he **snap**___ his fingers.

Billy **grab**___ the ball and **toss**___ it to Andy.

Chloe **dress**___ for school and **pack**___ her lunch.

3 Make a wall of *rhyming words*. Read them three times.

toss	m____	b____	gl____	cr____
mess	dr____	pr____	l____	bl____

MEMORY TRAINING

In your notebook, write the words you can remember. Check. Write your score here.

....

TARGETING SPELLING 1 © PASCAL PRESS ISBN 9781925490190

The verbs **am**, **is** and **are** show *present time* (NOW).
*Examples: I **am** six years old. Jill **is** sleepy. We **are** happy.*
The verbs **was** and **were** show *past time*.
*Examples: The bus **was** late, so the children **were** late for school.*

4 Colour the correct word in the brackets.

The horses [is are] in the paddock.

Olivia [was were] with her best friend.

I [am is] a good swimmer.

The dog [is was] lost for five days.

The men [was were] at the golf club yesterday.

The letters **-ing** can be added to many **verbs**. *Examples: go, go**ing**; do, do**ing**; play, play**ing**; pick, pick**ing**; smell, smell**ing**.*

5 Add -ing to each of these *verbs*.

kiss ________________ cross ________________

press ________________ miss ________________

toss ________________ dress ________________

The verbs **am**, **is**, **are**, **was** and **were** are also **'helping'** verbs.
They help verbs ending in **-ing** to show present and past time.
*Examples: I **am going** to the park. It **was raining** hard.*
*We **were playing** chess. They **are kicking** the football.*

am, is, are,
was and were
can help other
verbs.
(helping verbs)

6 Add a *helping verb* to complete each verb.

Liam ________ **licking** his sticky fingers.

The boys ________ **playing** in the sand yesterday.

The children ________ **crossing** the road with the teacher.

I ________ **going** home and they ________ **going** to the park.

UNIT 18

Word Endings: -ll

Some words end in **-ll**. If they are nouns, add **-s** to make them plural. *Example: hill, hill***s**

If they are verbs, add **-s** when they follow *he*, *she* or *it*.

*Examples: I fall; he fall***s***; they call; she call***s**

SEE & SAY

tell	call
smell	fall
swell	ball

did
here
there

Write the *rhyming words* from the word wheels.

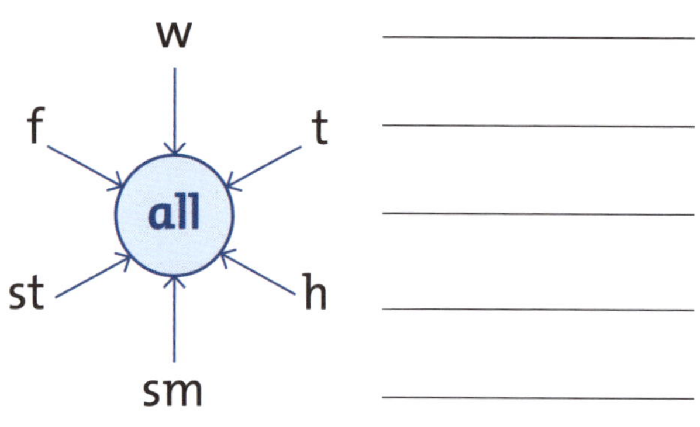

______
______
______
______
______
______

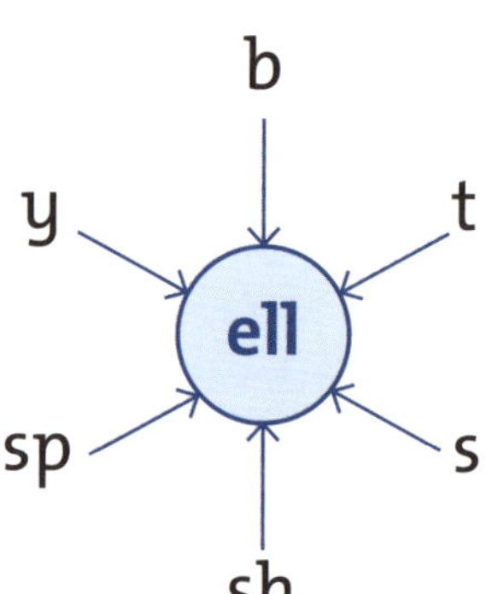

______
______
______
______
______
______

2 Add an ending to each of the words in bold to complete the sentences. Choose from -s, -es and -ing.

Jai is **call**______ for his **friend**______ to come and play.

The clown **toss**______ the **ball**______ into the air.

The leaves are **fall**______ off the tall **tree**______.

The **clock**______ in the hall are **tick**______.

TARGETING SPELLING 1 © PASCAL PRESS ISBN 9781925490190

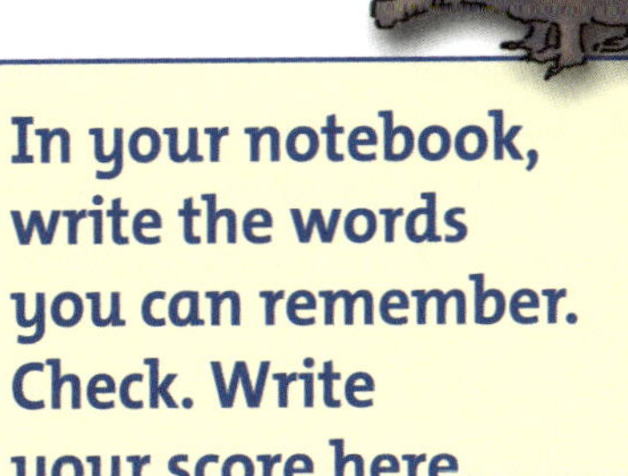

MEMORY TRAINING

3 Make a wall of *rhyming words*. Read them three times.

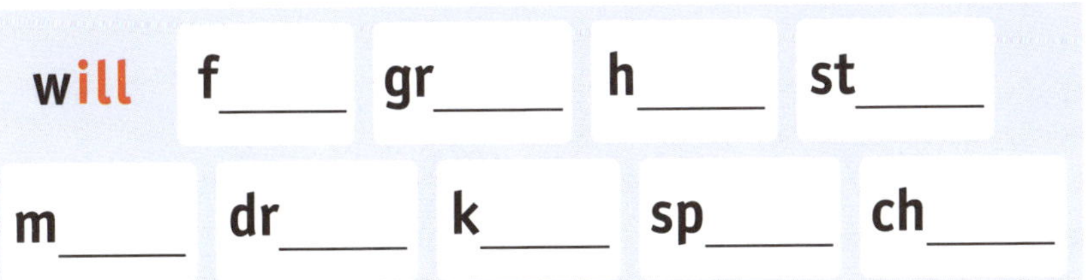

In your notebook, write the words you can remember. Check. Write your score here. ....

4 Write *adjectives* by adding **-y** to these nouns.

hill	____________	smell	____________	boss	____________
luck	____________	mess	____________	stick	____________
gloss	____________	rock	____________	sand	____________

5 Write a *helping verb* to complete each sentence.

We ________ **playing** cricket, but it began to rain.

They ________ **watching** a movie on TV tonight.

________ you **going** to the football game?

Dad ________ **selling** my old bike this Saturday.

I ________ **grilling** meat on the BBQ for lunch today.

am, is, are, was and were help other verbs to show when things are happening.

A helping verb followed by **not** can be joined together.

Examples: *is not* = ***isn't*** *was not* = ***wasn't***

are not = ***aren't*** *were not* = ***weren't***

These words are called **contractions**.

6 Write a *contraction* for the words in **bold**.

My brother **is not** playing for the red team. ____________

Dad said we **were not** to run in the hall. ____________

The man **was not** calling for help. ____________

We **are not** going to school by bus today. ____________

UNIT 19

Final Consonant Blends: -st

Many words end in -st, as in ***rest*** and ***pest***. If they are nouns, add -s to make them plural. *Examples: **nests, crusts***
If they are verbs, add -s when they follow *he, she* or *it*.
*Examples: I rest, he **rests**, she **rests**, it **rests***
Add -s to nouns to make them plural. *Examples: **tests**, **fists**, **vests***.
Note how we blend the two consonant sounds together when we say these words.

SEE & SAY

best	**fast**
test	**past**
west	**last**

then
they
sky

1 Choose a word from the *See and Say* list to complete each sentence.

Liam ran ________ the finishing line in first place.

Terry came ________ in the race.

The sun sets in the ________.

At school, I sit beside my ________ friend.

2 Add endings to the words in bold. Choose from -s, -ing and -y.

Magpies are **nest**_____ in the **tree**_____ in the park.

Jon is **toss**_____ **crust**_____ of bread to the **duck**_____.

This morning was **mist**_____ and **chill**_____.

Caleb is **rest**_____ before he **swim**_____ his last race.

3 Colour the pairs of words that are *opposite* in meaning. Use a different colour for each pair.

here	west	fast	tall	lost	first
short	last	there	found	slow	east

TARGETING SPELLING 1 © PASCAL PRESS ISBN 9781925490190

Run your finger down the *letter slide*.
Write the word under each slide.

l i st	tw i st	l o st	c o st
____	____	____	____

Write the *rhyming words*. Read them three times.

nest	dust
p	g
r	r
ch	m
v	j
qu	cr

MEMORY TRAINING

In your notebook, write the words you can remember. Check. Write your score here.

....

Add **-ed** to most verbs to show *past time*.
*Examples: test, test**ed**; call, call**ed**; toss, toss**ed***

Add **-ed** to each *verb* to show past time.

spill ____ rest ____ twist ____

smell ____ kick ____ crush ____

Build *adjectives* by adding **-y** to these nouns.

dust ____ frost ____ rust ____

gust ____ mist ____ crust ____

UNIT 20

Final Consonant Blends: -ng

Many words end in -ng. Some belong to the -ing word family. *Examples:* ***ring, sing, thing.***
Some belong to the -ang word family.
Examples: ***rang, sang, hang.***

SEE & SAY

ring	rang
wing	hang
sing	sang

now
how
or

Choose a word from the *See and Say* list to complete each sentence.

Mum will ________ the wet clothes on the line.

The children like to ________ the school song.

An eagle has two large ________s.

The bell ________ and we went into school.

Make a wall of *rhyming words.* Read them three times.

ring	k____	th____	sw____	st____
br____	cl____	sl____	str____	spr____

MEMORY TRAINING

In your notebook, write the words you can remember. Check. Write your score here.

....

3 Add -s, -es or -ing to the *verbs* in bold.

The school bell is **ring**_____ loudly.

Mike **swing**_____ his bat and **hit**_____ the ball hard.

The horse **swish**_____ its tail and **toss**_____ its mane.

The children are **bring**_____ their pets to school today.

A man **fall**___ from his boat and **cling**___ to the side.

TARGETING SPELLING 1 © PASCAL PRESS ISBN 9781925490190

Write each of these nouns in *plural* form.

ring ____________ fang ____________

string ____________ wing ____________

thing ____________ king ____________

Some *past tense* (time) verbs have a **special** form.
(We ***do not*** add **-ed**.)
*Examples: Today I **swim**. Yesterday I **swam**.*
*Today I **sing**. Yesterday I **sang**.*

Match the *present* and *special past* time verbs.

Present	Special past	Present	Special past
sing	came	do	hung
ring	sang	sting	sold
come	went	sell	did
go	rang	hang	stung

6 Choose the correct *consonant blend* to complete each word. Choose from cr, tr or st.

The car ____**ashed** into a tall green ____**ee**.

The horse ____**ots** along the dusty ____**ack**.

The ____**ucks** all ____**op** before they ____**oss** the bridge.

Don't ____**ep** on any ____**abs** in the sand.

7 Circle the *spelling mistake*. Write it correctly on the line.

Mum hang my socks on the line. ____________

The big bird flaps its winges. ____________

I singed a song to the class. ____________

A tiger runs very farst. ____________

TARGETING SPELLING 1 © PASCAL PRESS ISBN 9781925490190

UNIT 21

Final Consonant Blends: -ng

Many words end in **-ng**. Some belong to the **-ong** word family. *Examples: so**ng**, lo**ng**, wro**ng**.*
Some belong to the **-ung** word family.
*Examples: ru**ng**, su**ng**, hu**ng**.*
Add **-s** to nouns to make them plural.
*Examples: song**s**, lung**s**, gong**s**.*

SEE & SAY

song	hung
long	rung
along	stung

eight
good
make

1 **Choose a word from the *See and Say* list to complete the sentences.**

I got __________ by a bee.

They rode their bikes __________ the dusty road.

Peta has __________ black hair.

Jack __________ his hat on a hat peg.

2 **Add *consonants* to make some criss-cross words.**

	th	
sw	i	ng
	ng	

	i	ng
	ng	

	a	ng
	ng	

	o	ng
	ng	

	u	ng
	ng	

3 **Write each *number* as a word.**

1 __________ 2 __________ 3 __________ 4 __________

5 __________ 6 __________ 7 __________ 8 __________

TARGETING SPELLING 1 © PASCAL PRESS ISBN 9781925490190

UNIT 21

4 Colour the correct word in the brackets.

Ben [swing swung] his bat and hit the ball.

Last night, we [sing sang] in the school concert.

I will [ring rung] the bell at the end of the game.

Dad [hang hung] a picture on the wall.

Ants bite and bees [sting stung].

5 Add endings to the *verbs* in bold. Choose from -s, -es, -ing or -ed.

The monkeys are **swing**_____ through the treetops.

Molly **sing**_____ and **dance**_____, and **play**_____ the piano.

I **bump**_____ my glass and **spill**_____ the milk.

Sally **dress**_____ herself and **make**_____ her bed.

Are you **bring**_____ your dog with you?

WORD TRAPS

Don't mix up **eight** (8) and **ate**.
*Examples: I saw **eight** (8) hens and **eight** (8) ducks.*
*I **ate** an apple. Tom **ate** a peach.*

Don't mix up **buy** and **by**.
*Examples: You **buy** things at a shop. I came **by** bus.*
*Stand **by** the door. I went **by** his house.*

6 Colour the pairs of words that are *opposite* in meaning. Use a different colour for each pair.

long	good	small	buy	stop	in
sell	out	bad	go	short	big

7 Unscramble this sentence. Start with the word in bold.

flying **Jess** saw in plane a sky. the

____.

Final Consonant Blends: -nd

Many words end in **-nd**, as in ***hand*** and ***send***.
If they are nouns, add **-s** to make them plural.
Examples: hands, ponds, funds
If they are verbs, add **-s** when they follow *he*, *she* or *it*.
Examples: I bend, he bends, she bends, it bends

SEE & SAY

send	band
mend	sand
lend	grand

- give
- live
- them

1 Choose a word from the *See and Say* list to complete each sentence.

I play the drums in the school __________.

Will you __________ me five dollars, please?

I can't __________ the broken toy.

We look for shells on the __________ at the beach.

2 Write these nouns in *plural* form.

hand	__________	thing	__________	class	__________
song	__________	pond	__________	brand	__________

3 Build *adjectives* by adding -y to these nouns.

hand	__________	gloss	__________	rock	__________
sand	__________	mist	__________	hill	__________
wind	__________	smell	__________	trick	__________

TARGETING SPELLING 1 © PASCAL PRESS ISBN 9781925490190

Run your finger down the *letter slide*.
Write the word under each slide.

h / a / nd	l / a / nd	st / a / nd	br / a / nd
hand	______	______	______

b / e / nd	sp / e / nd	p / o / nd	f / o / nd
______	______	______	______

Add -ing or -ed to complete the *verbs*.

Mum is **mend**______ a hole in my jeans.

The teacher **hand**______ my book back to me.

Mel got **dress**______ and **brush**______ her hair.

Sasha is **play**______ the piano and Clare is **sing**______.

Match the *present* and *special past* time verbs.

Present	Special past	Present	Special past
bend	lent	give	stood
send	spent	come	made
lend	bent	stand	gave
spend	sent	make	came

Colour the correct *pronoun* in the brackets.

[They Them] are playing with [their there] trucks.

[He His] gran sent [he him] a birthday gift.

[She Her] lent [me my] a pencil.

[Us We] watched [they them] play football.

Final Consonant Blends: -nt

Many words end in -nt, as in ***tent*** and ***sent***.
If they are nouns, add -s to make them plural.
Examples: ants, tents, hints
If they are verbs, add -s when they follow *he*, *she* or *it*.
Examples: I pant, he pants, she pants, it pants

ant	went
pant	sent
plant	tent

take
home
nine

1 Choose a word from the *See and Say* list to complete each sentence.

We camp in a __________ in the summer holidays.

Dad will __________ an apple tree in our garden.

The children __________ to the zoo in a big bus.

A green __________ bit me on my big toe.

2 Name the pictures.

TARGETING SPELLING 1 © PASCAL PRESS ISBN 9781925490190

UNIT 23

3 Run your finger down the *letter slide*.
Write the word under each slide.

gr a nt	sl a nt	sp e nt	v e nt
grant	______	______	______
d i nt	h i nt	bl u nt	gr u nt
______	______	______	______

Make a wall of *rhyming words*. Read them three times.

nine	m____	sh____	d____	f____
l____	p____	v____	w____	sp____

MEMORY TRAINING

In your notebook, write the words you can remember. Check. Write your score here.

....

Add endings to the words in **bold**.
Choose from **-ing** and **-ed**.

John **sprint**______ past the finishing line.

The farmer is **plant**______ wheat.

The pigs are **grunt**______ and **roll**______ in the mud.

Eric **puff**______ and **pant**______ after his long run.

The windows are **glint**______ in the sun.

Put a line between each word in these *compound words*.

Examples: **pig|pen** **sun|set**

hillside grandmother hatband songbird

windmill football grandstand sandhill

If you were granted two wishes, what would they be?

1 ____

2 ____

Final Consonant Blends: -nk

Many words end in **-nk**, as in ***pink*** and ***wink***.
If they are nouns, add **-s** to make them plural.
*Examples: **banks**, **tanks**, **bunks***
If they are verbs, add **-s** when they follow *he*, *she* or *it*.
*Examples: I sink, he **sinks**, she **sinks**, it **sinks***

SEE & SAY

pink	**bank**
sink	**thank**
blink	**drank**

of
put
was

1 Choose a word from the *See and Say* list to complete each sentence.

I _________ a can of lemonade.

We had a picnic on the _________ of the river.

I can _________ my eyes very fast.

Put the dishes in the _________.

Add endings to the words in bold. Choose from -s, -ing and -ed.

The teacher **thank**______ me for my hard work.

The ship is **sink**______ into the sea.

The rain has **fill**______ the **tank**______ with water.

Brad is **think**______ about his **miss**______ dog.

Match the *present* and *special past* time verbs.

Present	Special past	Present	Special past
sink	thought	go	took
stink	drank	buy	was
drink	sank	take	went
think	stank	is	bought

TARGETING SPELLING 1 © PASCAL PRESS ISBN 9781925490190

Run your finger down the *letter slide*. Write the word under each slide.

t a nk	y a nk	tr u nk	ch u nk
tank			

w i nk	st i nk	th i nk	dr i nk

Add a *vowel* to mend the broken words (a, e, i, o, u).

An elephant has a long **tr__nk.**

I **dr__nk** a glass of water after my **l__ng** run.

My brother and I sleep in **b__nk b__ds.**

I ate **cr__ckers** and a big **ch__nk** of cheese.

The boat **s__nk** when it hit the **r__cks.**

Put a line between each word in these *compound words*.

Examples: **pig|pen sun|set**

junkyard	grandfather	netball	riverbank
homework	sandbank	takeaway	hairbrush

Now, choose two words and write a sentence for each one.

1 ______________________________

2 ______________________________

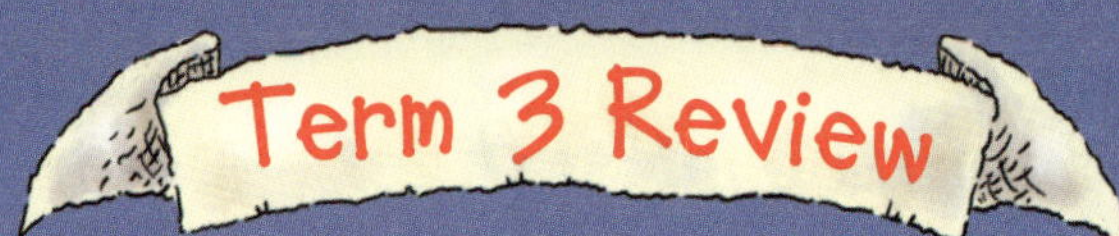

Term 3 Review

1 Name the pictures.

2 Write these nouns in *plural* form.

band ____________ wing ____________ test ____________

song ____________ cross ____________ thing ____________

dish ____________ doll ____________ glass ____________

3 Complete this table of *verbs*.

	Add -s or -es	Add -ing	Add -ed
call			
press			
thank			
twist			

4 Write each *number* as a word.

1 __________ 2 __________ 3 __________ 4 __________ 5 __________

6 __________ 7 __________ 8 __________ 9 __________ 10 __________

TARGETING SPELLING 1 © PASCAL PRESS ISBN 9781925490190

5 Write the *special past* time verbs.

Today I ...	Yesterday I ...
sing	
go	
send	

Today I ...	Yesterday I ...
do	
give	
is	

6 Write words of *opposite* meaning.

slow ____________ first ____________ short ____________

here ____________ bad ____________ on ____________

7 Add an ending to complete the words in bold.

Mum is **mend**______ the **hole**______ in my **sock**______.

Dad **plant**______ two apple **tree**______ and six rose **bush**______.

The children are **play**______ on the **sand**______ beach.

The horse **kick**______ up its heels and **toss**______ its mane.

It is a **frost**______ morning and the air is **chill**______.

8 Join the word parts to make *compound words*.

grand	work	junk	hill
wind	mother	net	stand
home	ball	sand	yard
foot	mill	grand	ball

9 Circle the *spelling mistakes*. Write the correct words on the lines.

The teacher ringed the school bell. ____________

The children bring them pets to school. ____________

Sally hanged her picture on the wall. ____________

There are ate boys in my class. ____________

UNIT 25

Final Consonant Blends: -mp

Many words end in **-mp**, as in *lamp* and *jump*.
If they are nouns, add **-s** to make them plural.
Examples: lamps, bumps, pumps
If they are verbs, add **-s** when they follow *he*, *she* or *it*.
Examples: I jump, he jumps, she jumps, it jumps

SEE & SAY

lamp	jump
damp	lump
ramp	stump

any
many
came

1 Choose a word from the *See and Say* list to complete the sentences.

A grasshopper can __________ a long way.

I pushed the boat down the __________ into the water.

I'm sitting on the __________ of a gum tree.

Wipe away the dust with a __________ cloth.

I have a bedside __________ so I can read in bed.

2 Write the *rhyming words*.

l**amp**	b**ump**
c	d
sc	h
cl	p
st	sl
tr	cl

3 Build *adjectives* by adding **-y** to these nouns.

bump __________

chunk __________

lump __________

grump __________

TARGETING SPELLING 1 © PASCAL PRESS ISBN 9781925490190

Add endings to the words in bold. Choose from -s, -ing and -ed.

Many people were **tramp**_____ through the snow.

The horse **jump**_____ the fence and ran away.

Our windmill **pump**_____ water and **fill**_____ our tanks.

I fell off my bike and **bump**_____ my head.

Many people like to go **camp**_____ in summer.

Write the *special past* time verbs and find them in the word search.

Today I ...	Yesterday I ...
come	
give	
see	
sing	
go	

t	h	i	w	n	g
c	a	m	e	k	a
s	t	o	n	s	v
l	p	z	t	a	e
w	a	s	b	n	r
a	g	d	l	g	v

Colour the letter before the correct answer to spell out the special message.

As night came, Dad lit the ___.	t	lump	c	lamp
A camel has one or two ___.	h	humps	r	hands
He gave me a ___ on the back.	a	thump	e	thumb
___ lots of water on hot days.	a	Drank	m	Drink
Jay has a ___ on his head.	p	bump	s	bunk
Don't ___ rubbish in the street.	u	damp	i	dump
Birds are singing in the ___ of trees.	r	clamp	o	clump
Clap your hands and ___ your feet.	n	stamp	e	stump

You are a ___ ___ ___ ___ ___ ___ ___ ___.

UNIT 26

Final Consonant Blends: -ft, -ff

Many words end in -ft as in *lift* and *left*, and -ff as in *puff* and *stuff*. If they are nouns, add -s to make them plural.
Examples: gifts, cuffs.
If they are verbs, add -s when they follow *he*, *she* or *it*. *Examples: I lift; he lifts, she lifts, it lifts; I puff; he puffs, she puffs, it puffs*

SEE & SAY

lift	stuff
left	stiff
soft	gruff

red
blue
green

1 Choose a word from the *See and Say* list to complete each sentence.

Holly cannot ________ the heavy box of books.

The old window latch is rusty and ________.

I have a ball in my ________ hand.

My kitten has ________ white fur.

2 Make a wall of *rhyming words*. Read them three times.

lift	g____	sh____	dr____	sw____
stuff	p____	m____	c____	fl____

MEMORY TRAINING

In your notebook, write the words you can remember. Check. Write your score here.

....

3 Write a word of *opposite* meaning to the word in bold.

We saw **large** animals and ________ animals at the zoo.

Look to the **right** and ________ then cross the street.

I have a ________ rope. Toby has a **short** one.

Nuts are **hard**, but jelly is ________.

TARGETING SPELLING 1 © PASCAL PRESS ISBN 9781925490190

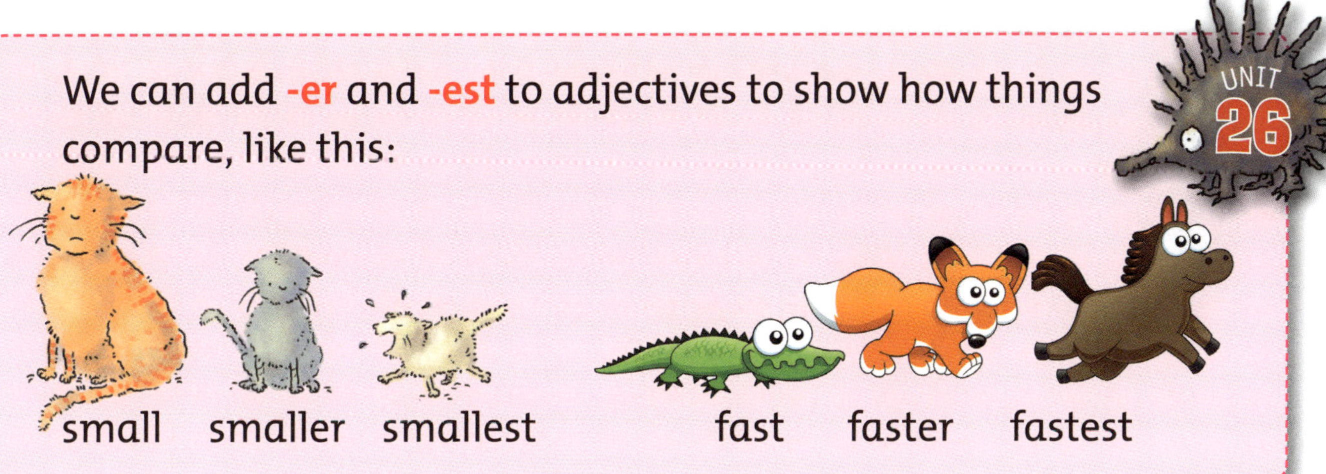

We can add **-er** and **-est** to adjectives to show how things compare, like this:

small smaller smallest fast faster fastest

4 Complete this table of *adjectives*.

	Add -er	Add -est
long		
quick		
cold		
small		

5 Add an ending to complete the words in **bold**.

A boat is **drift**_____ down the river.

Jamie is **puff**_____ and **pant**_____ after his long run.

I **lift**_____ the **fluff**_____ yellow chicken out of its nest.

I **open**_____ all my birthday **gift**_____.

6 Colour the correct word in the brackets.

Can I help you [left lift] that box?

We will [stuff stiff] the old rags into a bag.

Please [swift shift] your chair a little to the left.

Jan wore a [cuff muff] to keep her hands warm.

7 Write a sentence about a *gift* you have been given.

____

____

Final Consonant Blends: -tch

Many words end in **-tch** such as *pitch* and *catch*.
If they are nouns, add **-es** to make them plural.
Examples: patches, matches
If they are verbs, add **-es** when they follow *he*, *she* or *it*.
Examples: I catch, he (she or it) catches

SEE & SAY

catch	pitch
patch	witch
match	stitch

keep
out
ask

Choose a word from the *See and Say* list to complete each sentence.

This book is about a kind ________ and her cat.

Dan is playing in a football ________ today.

Cricket is played on a cricket ________.

Mum will stitch a ________ on my torn pants.

2 Write the *rhyming words* from the word wheel. Read them three times.

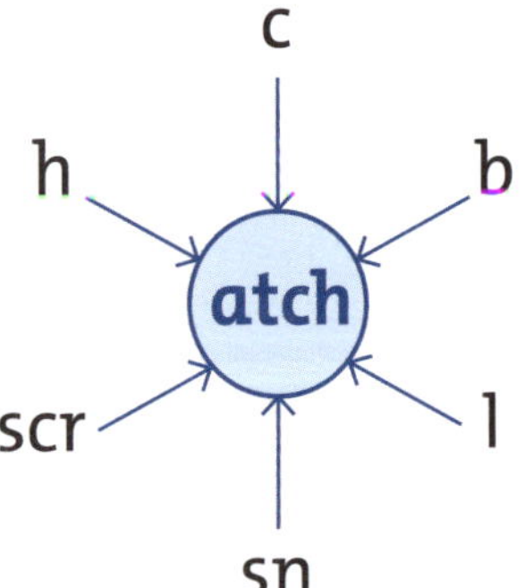

____
____
____
____
____
____

MEMORY TRAINING

In your notebook, write the words you can remember. Check. Write your score here.

....

3 Make a wall of *rhyming words*.

keep	sh____	d____	j____	sl____
p____	w____	st____	cr____	b____

TARGETING SPELLING 1 © PASCAL PRESS ISBN 9781925490190

Add an ending to complete the words in bold. Choose from -s, -es, -ing and -ed.

Harry needs **crutch**_____ to help him walk.

Jon **catch**_____ a bus to school on **Friday**_____.

Sam is **clutch**_____ his ball in his **hand**_____.

A small yellow chick **hatch**_____ out of the egg.

Six football **match**_____ will be played this month.

Build *adjectives* by adding -y to these nouns.

itch __________ fluff __________ bump __________

patch __________ scruff __________ grump __________

Find the *colours* in the word search.

red
blue
pink
green
yellow

t	w	p	i	n	k
f	g	s	r	i	n
l	r	o	b	s	g
y	e	l	l	o	w
y	e	k	u	w	b
l	n	r	e	d	p

Colour the correct word in the brackets.

Andy will [patch pitch] the ball to the batter.

Did the cat [scratch snatch] your arm?

I don't know [witch which] way to go.

The chicks will soon [hatch hitch] out of the eggs.

[Crutch Catch] the ball and don't let go.

Final Consonant Blends: -nch

Many words end in **-nch**, as in *pinch* and *munch*.
If they are nouns, add **-es** to make them plural.
Examples: branches, lunches
If they are verbs, add **-es** when they follow *he*, *she* or *it*.
Examples: I munch, he (she or it) munches.

SEE & SAY

lunch	bunch
punch	bench
crunch	branch

day
say
saw

1 Write these nouns in *plural* form.

bunch	____________	lunch	____________
punch	____________	branch	____________
bench	____________	finch	____________

- Say the words three times.
- How many can you remember?
- Write them in your notebook. Check.
- Write your score here.

....

2 Make a wall of *rhyming words*. Read them three times.

day	s____	p____	m____
l____	h____	b____	w____
pl____	sw____	st____	tr____

3 Draw a picture for each *compound word*.

sandcastle	playtime	lunchbox

TARGETING SPELLING 1 © PASCAL PRESS ISBN 9781925490190

Colour the correct word in the brackets.

I gave my teacher a [punch bunch] of flowers.

Jacob will [pinch pitch] the ball to the batter.

We sat on a park [bench bunch] to watch the ducks.

Ella broke her leg and needs [crunches crutches].

Add an ending to complete the words in bold.

He hits the **punch**_____ bag with his fists.

People on the park **bench**_____ are eating their **lunch**_____.

Kenny **clench**_____ his fists in anger.

We ate some **crunch**_____ red apples.

I **scrunch**_____ up the paper and **toss**_____ it in the bin.

We sometimes add **-er** to verbs to name people who do certain things.

*Examples: Someone who pitches a ball is a pitch**er**.*

*Someone who catches a ball is a catch**er**.*

Add -er to name these people.

Someone who can **box** is a _______________.

Someone who can **jump** is a _______________.

Someone who can **hunt** is a _______________.

Someone who can **spell** is a _______________.

Someone who can **farm** is a _______________.

UNIT 29 Final Consonant Blends: -lf, -sp, -sk

Some words end in **-lf**, **-sp** and **-sk**.
Examples: golf, crisp, mask
Note how we blend the two consonant sounds together when we say these words.

SEE & SAY

self	shelf
wisp	crisp
task	mask

- little
- very
- next

1 Choose a word from the *See and Say* list to complete each sentence.

Put the book back on the __________, please.

Jake wore a clown __________ over his face.

It is Joe's __________ to hand out our sketch books.

There are little __________s of cloud in the sky.

2 Name the pictures.

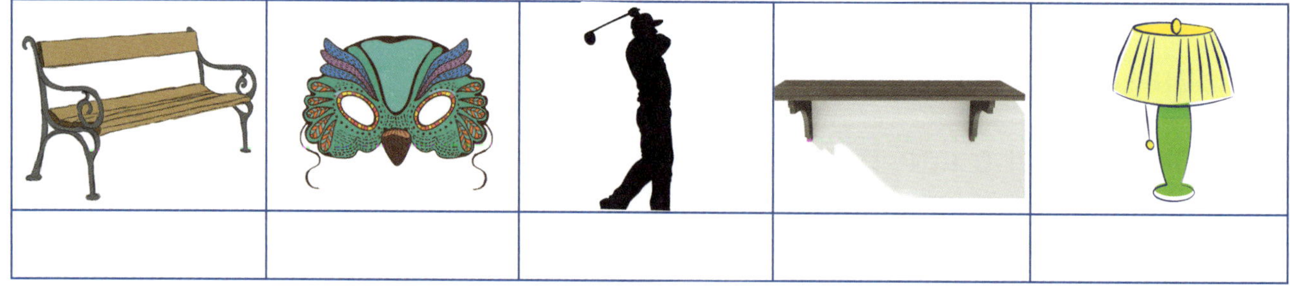

3 Write the *next number* in words.

after 1 __________	after 6 __________
after 2 __________	after 7 __________
after 3 __________	after 8 __________

TARGETING SPELLING 1 © PASCAL PRESS ISBN 9781925490190

UNIT 29

4 Add an ending to complete the words in bold.

The children are **crunch**______ through the crisp snow.

The teacher **ask**______ us to clean our **paintbrush**______.

Stan is **walk**______ to school by himself.

We saw **wisp**______ of smoke coming through the **tree**______.

When I **play**______ golf, I lost three golf **ball**______.

5 Colour the pairs of words that are *opposite* in meaning. Use a different colour for each pair.

over	little	boy	day	here	left
girl	right	there	big	under	night

6 Choose the correct *pronoun* to complete each sentence.

myself herself himself itself yourself

Bella looked at ____________ in the mirror.

Can you lift that heavy box by ____________?

I can make my bed and dress ____________.

A sheep stood by ____________ in a corner of the field.

Henry cut ____________ on a bit of glass.

7 Write each noun in *plural* form.

mask ____________

flask ____________

task ____________

desk ____________

risk ____________

basket ____________

The plural of *shelf* is ***shelves***
The plural of *self* is ***selves***.
*Examples: **ourselves**, **yourselves**, **themselves***

TARGETING SPELLING 1 © PASCAL PRESS ISBN 9781925490190

Word Endings

We add **endings** to words so that we can use them correctly in our writing.
Examples: *Jack likes fish**ing** and play**ing** with his Lego block**s**.*
The **endings** we add are **-s** or **-es**, **-ing**, **-ed**, **-y**, **-er** and **-est**.

Add -s or -es to write nouns in their plural form.
Add -s or -es to verbs that follow *she*, *he* or *it*.
Add -s *most of the time.*
Add -es to words that end in s, ss, sh, ch and x.

1 Add -s or -es to these *nouns* and *verbs*.

grub ______	bench ______	block ______
dress ______	ball ______	fox ______
fill ______	clap ______	munch ______
jump ______	smash ______	kiss ______

Add -ing, -ed, -y, -er or -est to words that have two letters after a short vowel. Examples: *jump, jumping; pant, panted; dust, dusty; sing, singer; soft, softer, softest*

2 Add endings to these words.

Add -ing	Add -ed	Add -y	Add -er	Add -est
miss	test	smell	sink	long
drink	bump	risk	sting	rich

TARGETING SPELLING 1 © PASCAL PRESS ISBN 9781925490190

If the word has only one letter after the vowel, you must ***double*** that letter before you add -ing, -ed, -y, -er or -est.
Examples: *run, ru**nn**ing; hop, ho**pp**ed; fun, fu**nn**y; big, bi**gg**er, bi**gg**est*

Double means write the same letter again.

Do you need to *double* a letter before adding -ing, -ed, -y, -er or -est? Write *yes* or *no* on the line.
Hint: Colour the vowel. Count the letters after it.

camp	__________	cut	__________	swim	__________
trot	__________	skip	__________	press	__________
rip	__________	trick	__________	grab	__________
long	__________	drop	__________	pump	__________

Add endings to these words. Use the *doubling rule*.
Hint: Colour the vowel. Count the letters after it.

Add -ing		Add -ed	
run		stop	
pack		crash	
skip		trip	
cut		jump	

Add -y		Add -er		Add -est	
mud		rich		long	
luck		wet		fat	
frost		thin		sad	
sun		soft		slim	

Letter Patterns: -igh

The letter pattern **igh** is an old word pattern with the sound of the letter **i**, as in ***high***, ***night*** and ***light***.
The **g** and **h** are *not* sounded, so you must remember what the words *look* like.

SEE & SAY

high	tight
night	light
might	right

every
open
down

1 Choose a word from the *See and Say* list to complete each sentence.

My belt is too ________.

I think it ________ rain tomorrow.

Allie writes with her ________ hand.

The plane is flying ________ in the sky.

MEMORY TRAINING

- Say the words three times.
- How many can you remember?
- Write them in your notebook. Check.
- Write your score here.

....

2 Make a wall of *rhyming words*. Read them three times.

might	n______	t______	l______
f______	fr______	s______	
sl______	r______	br______	

3 Compare the *adjectives*.

	Add -er	Add -est
light		
bright		
tight		

TARGETING SPELLING 1 © PASCAL PRESS ISBN 9781925490190

4 Name the pictures.

5 Colour the pairs of words that are *opposite* in meaning. Use a different colour for each pair.

bright	light	right	dark	night	tight
wrong	loose	day	heavy	dull	light

6 Add endings to the words in each list. Use the *doubling rule*. The vowels are in red to help you.

	Add -ing
pack	
run	
lift	
hop	
crash	

	Add -ed
slip	
tramp	
hum	
fill	
spot	

	Add -y
fun	
lump	
mud	
trick	
bag	

	Add -er	Add -est
thin		
wet		
big		
long		
fat		

UNIT 32 Letter Teams: ar

The letter **r** changes the sound of vowels.
It has an **ah** sound in words like *car*, *star* and *bark*.

SEE & SAY

car	card
far	yard
star	hard

- today
- old
- cold

1 Write the *rhyming words*. Read them three times.

art	park
c	m
d	d
sm	sh
st	b
ch	sp

MEMORY TRAINING

In your notebook, write the words you can remember. Check. Write your scores here.

....

2 Write these nouns in *plural* form.

car	________	cart	________	yard	________
star	________	shark	________	arm	________
park	________	jar	________	card	________

3 Name the pictures.

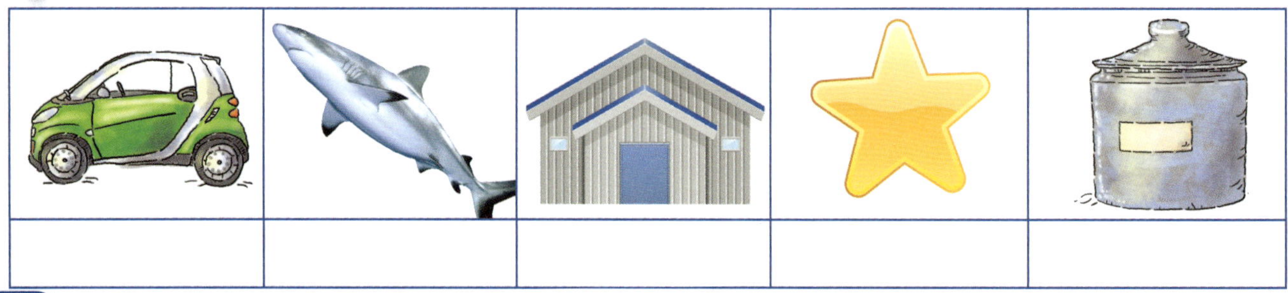

TARGETING SPELLING 1 © PASCAL PRESS ISBN 9781925490190

4 **Add an ending to complete the *verbs* in bold. Choose from -ing or -ed.**

The teacher **mark**_____ my work and **hand**_____ it back.

Butterflies are **dart**_____ about in my garden.

The movie **start**_____ at 7 o'clock.

The dogs are **bark**_____ and the cows are **run**_____.

I **jump**_____ the gate and **skip**_____ up the path.

5 **Colour a word on the top row and a word on the bottom row to make a compound word. Use a different colour for each compound word.**

art	park	high	moon	night	farm
yard	light	dress	way	work	land

6 **Add an ending to complete the words in bold. Choose from -er or -est.**

I think you are **smart**_____ than me.

Jenny has the **sharp**_____ pencil.

The sky got **dark**_____ and the wind got **strong**_____.

The chess game was the **hard**_____ one I've played.

7 **Write about a *birthday party* and draw a picture about it.**

____

____

____

____

____

____

____

TARGETING SPELLING 1 © PASCAL PRESS ISBN 9781925490190

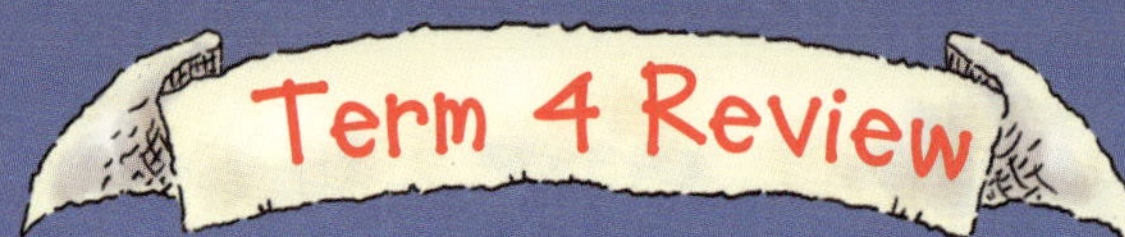

Name the pictures.

Write these nouns in *plural* form.

task ____________ lunch ____________ pump ____________

stitch ____________ lamp ____________ day ____________

gift ____________ box ____________ class ____________

Complete this table of *verbs*. *(Remember the doubling rule).*

	Add -s or -es	Add -ing	Add -ed
pump			
hop			
flash			
pat			

Write each *number* as a word.

1 ____________ 2 ____________ 3 ____________ 4 ____________ 5 ____________

6 ____________ 7 ____________ 8 ____________ 9 ____________ 10 ____________

TARGETING SPELLING 1 © PASCAL PRESS ISBN 9781925490190

Term 4 Review

5 Add -y to these words. *(Remember the doubling rule).*

bag ________ frost ________ fun ________

mist ________ mud ________ crunch ________

fog ________ skin ________ fluff ________

6 Write the *special past* time verbs.

Today I ...	Yesterday I ...
give	
run	
get	
go	

Today I ...	Yesterday I ...
do	
see	
fall	
sit	

7 Write words of *opposite* meaning.

big ________ left ________ short ________

over ________ low ________ day ________

first ________ hard ________ slow ________

8 Circle each *spelling mistake*. Write it correctly on the line.

Jane is skiping along the path. ________

Jason is tallest than me. ________

Today is hot and suny. ________

The horse jumpt over the fence. ________

9 Join the word parts to make *compound words*.

grand	box	moon	yard
book	stand	farm	stack
lunch	way	hay	shelf
high	mark	book	light

The Top 3 Spelling Rules

Rules	How to apply the rule	Examples
1 Doubling rule	When there is only ONE consonant after a short vowel, **double** that consonant before you add ***-ing***, ***-ed***, ***-y***, ***-er*** or ***-est***.	hop hopping skip skipped fun funny big bigger biggest
	If there are already TWO consonants after the short vowel, just add an ending.	jump jumping pack packed dust dusty rich richer richest
2 The *e* rule	When a word ends in ***e***, drop the ***e*** before adding an ending that begins with a vowel or ***y***.	ride riding shine shiny prickle prickly
	Do NOT drop the ***e*** when adding ***-ly*** (or any suffix beginning with a consonant).	safe safely safety use useful useless
3 The *y* rule	When a noun ends in ***y***, follow these simple rules to write its plural: 1 If the letter before the ***y*** is a vowel, just add ***-s***. 2 If the letter before the ***y*** is NOT a vowel, change ***y*** to ***i*** and add ***-es***.	 boys days monkeys baby babies lady ladies
	When a regular verb ends in ***y***, follow these simple rules to write it in present or past tense: 1 Just add ***-ing***. 2 If the letter before the ***y*** is a vowel, just add ***-s*** or ***-ed***. 3 If the letter before the ***y*** is NOT a vowel, change ***y*** to ***i*** and add ***-es*** or ***-ed***.	 fly flying carry carrying play plays played enjoy enjoys enjoyed cry cries cried hurry hurries hurried
	When an adjective ends in ***y***, change ***y*** to ***i*** and add ***-er*** or ***-est*** (comparing) and ***-ly*** (adverbs of manner).	happier happiest happily lazier laziest lazily

Common Endings

Ending	Purpose	Examples	Rule
-s	Add ***-s*** to MOST nouns to write them in plural form. Add ***-s*** to present tense verbs when the subject is *'he'*, *'she'* or *'it'*.	dogs apples toys hats runs plays rains growls eats stares swims	
-es	Add ***-es*** to nouns and verbs that end in ***s***, ***ss***, ***z***, ***zz***, ***x***, ***sh***, ***ch***.	buses dishes foxes tosses buzzes itches	
-ing	Add ***-ing*** to verbs to make present participles.	going jumping crying hopping rideing	1, 2, 3
-ed	Add ***-ed*** to *regular* verbs to make past participles.	planted clapped played carried baked	1, 2, 3
-y	Add ***-y*** to form adjectives.	bumpy funny stoney	1, 2
-er -est	Add ***-er*** or ***-est*** to show how adjectives and adverbs compare.	taller tallest bigger biggest busier busiest faster fastest	1, 2, 3
-ly	Add ***-ly*** to form adverbs of manner.	quickly lately noisily	2, 3

TARGETING SPELLING 1 © PASCAL PRESS ISBN 9781925490190